TO CONCERNED AMERICANS

Wisdom and Warning to Those Who Care For the Land of the Free

JOHN WHITE

CROSS STONE
PUBLISHING

CONTENTS

PREAMBLES

"If a kingdom is divided against itself, that kingdom cannot stand. And if a house is divided against itself, that house will not be able to stand."

Jesus quoted in Mark 3:24–25, NRSV[1]

GREAT IRONIES OF IGNORANCE

WE HAVE A GREAT COLLECTIVE KNOWLEDGE of our world, and a vast global, essentially instantaneous, communication network, yet much ignorance still exists.

The greatest economy ever in the world has a large portion of its population that is ignorant about how their own economy functions and why their nation is great.

The great advance of western societies, particularly in the United States, was made possible by the moral, ethical, righteous-minded, trustful foundation of the Christian faith guided by God-given standards, including the Golden Rule that enables well-rewarded innovation to flourish in a free-market economy. Many in the United States today are unaware of, or fail to recognize, the ultimate source of the vast largess which we presently enjoy but are rapidly consuming and destroying.

PREFACE

THIS BOOK BEGAN NOT AS A BOOK, but as an essay about a specific concern nearly twenty years ago. Over the next several years I felt led to write other essays, each time addressing a current event. Thus, much of the writing for this book occurred in "real time," with appropriate later edits to adjust time tenses to make sense to the reader. Some section titles contain a specific date identifying the time of the writing, not necessarily the time of the event described.

A few years ago, I felt a nudge that I should collect these writings into a book. As time went on, the nudge became a compelling force. During 2019, I thought I neared completion of the book. Then developments began to unfold that pointed to more reasons for this writing. The following year brought sea-changing crises that pointed me in additional directions with a greater sense of need and urgency. I hope knowing the history of this book helps you understand the organization and flow of the writing.

This book seeks to provide rational and moral bases for decision-making and solutions to problems we see in our nation. I include specific criticisms in places, but they are meant for learning, not as an attack toward others. We all have our flaws and mistakes, but what we do to learn from them and build from them is as important as successes we may have.

Throughout this book, I provide examples of solutions to various concerns, problems, and issues. A vast number of individuals in our nation possess various combinations of great knowledge, ingenuity, intuition, morality, wealth, intelligence, altruism, diligence, industry, determination, and faith. Recognizing and enabling their potential to focus on problems that concern us will lead to better and more efficient solutions than what one person like myself, or a small exclusive clique, may conceive.

I talk about ignorance. My comments are not meant as a criticism of any person or group. My remarks stem not only from observation of other individuals and our general populace but also from my own experience. Even while writing this book, on occasion, I'd write something that included an assumption, and then do research to check the facts behind my assumption and find my premise was not completely accurate.

We are all ignorant in various aspects of human knowledge. I possess knowledge and skills in some areas that are specific to my occupations that few others have. Most people do have some such specific knowledge. Possession of expertise in some fields does not make anyone all knowing.

However, there is a core of common knowledge critical for all members of an organization to possess and actively apply, enabling that organization to operate properly and effectively. To be successful, a company needs all employees endowed with a basic core of knowledge of proper procedures, safety rules, customer relations, administrative functions, and other items specific to their industry.

At the same time, businesses that are successful in the long term encourage innovative thought, "outside the box" thinking. Good employees in a thriving company are not automatons who mindlessly go about their work—they think about improving efficiency, quality, service, and productivity.

The same is true for a nation. We are a land built upon individual freedom with certain inalienable rights enumerated. However, with rights come responsibilities. Citizens of a nation that want to preserve their rights and freedoms must bear the responsibilities of maintaining their privileges. Freedom is not free. It requires acquisition of fundamental truths and knowledge, effort, and self-sacrifice.

Furthermore, individual rights are not boundless. My rights end where another person's rights begin.[2] There are many ways that we inadvertently cause losses of freedom, both individually and as a nation. This theme appears several times in this book.

Political divisions cause extremes to rule and divide, which hinders objective discourse. The meetings that led to the drafting of the Constitution were held by thoughtful, concerned men. They were all allowed to give voice to their opinions which drew upon their various experiences. Though there were party affiliations, the comments of the participants were guided primarily by their personal convictions and perspectives. They agonized over the wording of individual sentences. They had real debates, not strings of speeches driven by political posturing. Several chapters that follow point out the damaging effects of the political divisions and disconnects we witness today in our nation.

Fiscal responsibility is vital to maintaining a secure future for any entity, whether individuals, businesses, or governments. The economic principle of "Scarcity of Resources" guides necessary hard choices about what money should be spent on. We have arrived at the point where a vast number of people in the US do not understand this principle and fail to see the danger of unfettered spending. You will read about the explosion of unrestrained debt, new currency creation by our government, and the grave dangers these pose to our nation.

Finally, the founders recognized the importance of religious faith and education in the success of the brave new experiment that they recognized they were undertaking. They saw this new nation as a gift from God. They prophetically spoke of the need for Christian convictions to guide the hearts and minds of our nation's citizens and leaders. Without such convictions, this great experiment could not survive.

There are many today that look out on our great land and fear that we stand near the precipice where just a few missteps could send us falling with disastrous consequences. This book hopes to call us to avert that fall.

ON THE PRECIPICE

PORTIONS OF THIS BOOK HAVE BEEN in the making for many years, but as I begin to write on this day of May 11, 2019, I am certain most citizens of our United States of America agree that we are a nation deeply divided. An examination of our history shows that there have always been disagreements regarding how we should govern ourselves, and the nature and breadth of laws we should retain. But at this juncture in time, it feels particularly bitter and partisan beyond repair. Extreme views, misrepresentations, insults, and outright falsehoods put forth by politicians in place of facts, become reported by multiple media outlets without question or contrary opinion.

Decisions being made by many political leaders are guided not by sound reason and moral principles but upon one-sided opinion, special interests, party loyalties, and personal ambition. In the meantime, our nation is becoming overloaded by unprecedented and unrestrained debt. Our enemies gather and strengthen themselves, seemingly unnoticed by many of our lawmakers and most of our citizenry. The moral fundamentals that guided our nation for nearly two centuries are being attacked and dismantled.

There have been serious dividing issues intensely debated in our nation's past. The most bitter and divisive was that of slavery. At the founding of our nation, slavery was a contentious issue. Through the first seven decades of our republic, the issue of slavery grew to the point of all-out warfare, costing the lives of more than 600,000 strong, bright, and courageous young American men. There were many aspects and events that led to the American Civil War (1860–1865). There are a couple of things of importance to consider.

First, a great amount of misinformation was circulated and repeated regarding Abraham Lincoln. He was insulted and excoriated by the media, not just in southern states, but by northern sources as well.[3,4] Further, his position on the slave issue was mischaracterized. Lincoln was the presidential candidate for the Republican Political Party. Southerners before the election viewed Lincoln merely as a member of the "Black Republican Party," known to be anti-slavery.[5]

Although Lincoln won the presidential election held in 1860 in a four-way race, several southern states did not even place him on their ballots. Secession was a forgone conclusion for them if a Republican won the presidential election. This despite Lincoln's repeated insistence that he had no intention of interfering with slavery in states where it was already established.

To emphasize that point, he quoted from one of his published pre-election speeches during his first inaugural address, "I have no purpose, directly or indirectly, to interfere with the institution of slavery in the States where it exists. I believe I have no lawful right to do so, and I have no inclination to do so." Had southern politicians and media not judged Lincoln merely by party affiliation and critical political hyperbole, our nation might possibly have been spared its deadliest war.

Second, slavery was a moral issue. The arguments in favor of the slave trade included quotations of Biblical scriptures that appeared to condone and even support slavery. The enslavement of blacks was justified in their minds by the popular false notion of the time that blacks were an inferior race. Opposition by people in "free" states was seen by southerners as a potential threat to what they considered to be their *right* to own slaves.

The opposition to the slave trade was led by Christians who saw that institution as unjust and saw through any veiled attempts to justify slavery by quoting Scripture. For more than a hundred years before 1860, books and articles detailed the biblical basis for opposition to the slave trade.[6,7,8] In 1807 the importation of slaves to the United States had been outlawed. By 1827 five northern states had abolished slavery.

In 1834, Great Britain abolished slavery throughout most of its empire, an effort championed by William Wilberforce influenced and encouraged strongly by prominent Christians of his time. In 1852, Harriet Beecher Stowe's Uncle Tom's Cabin became the second best-selling book of the era behind the Bible. Her book depicted the tragic treatment of black slaves based upon her personal interviews with former slaves. Dozens of other autobiographies of former slaves had also been published by 1860, including two by Frederick Douglas, describing the dehumanizing hardships of the institution of slavery in the United States.

The opinion that it was proper for white men to own black slaves, and that it represented a constitutional right, was self-centered and bereft of honest morality and objective facts available to the public in 1860. Thus, their argument for continuing slavery was fundamentally driven by secular self-interest. The presence of a significant segment of the nation's citizens who turned a blind eye to the facts and morality of their stand on the issue led to the greatest loss of life by American soldiers in any war that the United States has fought.

I pray I am wrong, but it feels as if we are on the precipice of circumstances that can lead to equally dire consequences for our nation today. Indeed, our situation today is even more perilous. While we fail to recognize and deal with the underlying economic, civil, and moral decay of our nation, many groups, and nations, both within our borders and around the world, anxiously await and prepare for the opportunity to bring destruction upon us. To avert a tragic national fall, we must learn from our past and recognize the need to decide the issues we face based upon what is morally right and factually correct and not from our own self-centered interests.

CHAPTER 1

THE SOUL OF A NATION

"Of all the dispositions and habits which lead to political prosperity, religion and morality are indispensable supports. In vain would that man claim the tribute of patriotism, who should labor to subvert these great pillars of human happiness, these firmest props of the duties of men and citizens. The mere politician, equally with the pious man, ought to respect and to cherish them . . . . And let us with caution indulge the supposition that morality can be maintained without religion. Whatever may be conceded to the influence of refined education on minds of peculiar structure, reason and experience both forbid us to expect that national morality can prevail in exclusion of religious principle."

George Washington, Farewell Address 1796

"From this day forward, the millions of our school children will daily proclaim in every city and town, every village and rural school house, the dedication of our nation and our people to the Almighty . . . . In this way we are reaffirming the transcendence of religious faith in America's heritage and future; in this way we shall constantly strengthen those spiritual weapons which forever will be our country's most powerful resource, in peace or in war."

Dwight D. Eisenhower, on Flag Day June 14, 1954, the day he signed into law a Joint Resolution of Congress amending the Pledge of Allegiance to include the phrase "under God."

"In the beginning when God created the heavens and the earth . . ."

Genesis 1:1, NRSV

BEGINNING

I am convinced that a book of this nature cannot begin without first establishing the most fundamental requirement for a free, thriving, and sustainable society. That requirement is the belief and acceptance by citizens of God, creator of the universe.

When confronted by the recognition of that power greater than ourselves, the living God, creator of the universe, we cannot help but be humbled. Humility before God is essential for a person in authority to constrain the human tendency toward considering oneself greater than others. Humility counters the lust for power and control over the lives of fellow citizens.

Humility before God is the fundamental from which grows the attitude of the servant leader. Such leaders see their role as public servants chosen or designated to serve their constituents rather than as overlords dictating to those beneath them how they should live. Humility keeps the focus on what is best for the citizens, and away from self-serving actions designed merely to maintain the arrogant in power.

In an address to the Templeton Society in London in 1983, Aleksandr Solzhenitsyn made this point using his own experiences in the Soviet Union as an example. He stated, "Over a half century ago, while I was still a child, I recall hearing a number of old people offer the following explanation for the great disasters that had befallen Russia: 'Men have forgotten God; that's why all this has happened.' Since then I have spent well-nigh fifty years working on the history of our revolution; in the process I have read hundreds of books, collected hundreds of personal testimonies, and have already contributed eight volumes of my own toward the effort of clearing away the rubble left by that upheaval. But if I were asked today to formulate as concisely as possible the main cause of the ruinous revolution that swallowed up some sixty million of our people, I could not put it more accurately than to repeat: 'Men have forgotten God; that's why all this has happened.'"[9]

Many politicians may claim God, and even Christ, but too often they do so vainly. They make the claim merely to gather power and supporters unto themselves. In the public political arena this creates the need for discernment among voters. On more than one occasion Jesus teaches about discerning between good and bad individuals using the analogy of discerning good and bad trees by the fruits they produce:

"Beware of false prophets, who come to you in sheep's clothing but inwardly are ravenous wolves. You will know them by their fruits. Are grapes gathered from thorns, or figs from thistles?

In the same way, every good tree bears good fruit, but the bad tree bears bad fruit. A good tree cannot bear bad fruit, nor can a bad tree bear good fruit. Every tree that does not bear good fruit is cut down and thrown into the fire. Thus you will know them by their fruits." (Matthew 7:15-20, NRSV).

In the above passage, Jesus warns us of those who distort truth to get us to follow them. We should not judge them by what they claim they will do for us, but by what they have done in the past and have accomplished. Further, do they sincerely give credit to God and others for what they accomplish, or do they claim the credit unto themselves? Paul briefly describes what is required for discernment and why it is needed:

"Do not be conformed to this world, but be transformed by the renewing of your minds, so that you may discern what is the will of God—what is good and acceptable and perfect." (Romans 12:2, NRSV).

The transformation Paul describes calls us in part to refocus our attention on what God would have us do for him and others, rather than on what we want for ourselves. From this perspective, for those in a government leadership role, executive or legislative decisions should be based upon what is best for all citizens, rather than what is best for an individual's career, a political party, or a special interest. Thoughtful consideration of positions other than your own special interest is required for discernment.

What is best for all citizens may not always be what you might think. In some of the chapters that follow, you may be surprised and challenged in some of your preconceived notions of what is best and right for citizens, leaders, and a government to do and not do.

IN GOD WE TRUST

A free and thriving society can only exist when citizens are spiritually and morally united and guided by standards that imbue mutual trust and cooperation without tyrannical threat and force. Since the Civil War, the phrase "In God We Trust" has been placed on most coins struck by the US mint. The need for faith and trust is vital for a free society to function. When you go on the internet to buy a product, you trust that what you order and pay for will be of the type and quality that was advertised, and that it will be delivered in a timely fashion. If that trust did not exist, the internet market could not function.

The same is true for all other transactions, whether it is a car, a television or a fast-food meal. No trade can proceed without the purchaser being able to trust the seller to provide a reasonable product, and the seller trusting that the currency provided can be relied upon.[10] It is no accident that Americans, through many generations, acknowledge our collective trust in God on our currency. The great economic success of the United States since the Civil War has been made possible by that trust.

Trust is also an essential component for a government to exist and function. Many of the original framers of the Constitution did not have a great trust in a strong central government and feared that it could be easily abused and usurped. I have several quotes of original founders throughout this book that attest to this concern. As time goes on, I see more and more the wisdom of their mistrust. They were careful and deliberate in crafting a constitution that would limit the ability of untrustworthy individuals to abuse the authority of a federal government. Even with the best-written constitution, it is still necessary that citizens can trust individuals in authority to enforce and abide by duly enacted legislation, and act in the best interest of the people they serve.

For our free society to exist, citizens in general, and authorities in particular, must be considered trustworthy. From the janitor to Congress and the president, trust is necessary for a free society to function. The fundamentals of the Christian faith call upon followers to be, among other things, trustworthy. Those fundamentals have been woven into the fabric of American culture. Those teachings of a moral higher authority, a God who values others over self and promotes the pursuit of justice and mercy.

American voters appear to subconsciously value the acceptance of a higher authority in God when considering their choice for president. All presidents in the history of our nation acknowledged a belief in God. Further regarding Christian faith, all but two or three of our forty-five presidents professed some manner of Christianity.

There are many in our society today that espouse portions of the fundamentals of Christian faith while ignoring or denying their original source. This is a convenience that allows them to claim some moral authority without conceding and submitting to a higher authority. The society that adopts this view places itself on a descending slope where everyone is enabled to choose for themselves what is morally right. The moral fabric binding that society together is thus undone. Laws by themselves do not constrain the human heart. Without the constraint of a faith in God, human nature will ultimately degenerate into self-serving attitudes counter to what is best for all involved. At the beginning of this chapter, I quote George Washington from his 1796 farewell address. He warned us over 200 years ago of the danger of a morality in the absence of religious principles.

On July 11, 1955, a bill was signed into law by President Eisenhower requiring "In God We Trust" to be placed on all money produced by the US treasury. The call for "In God We Trust" by the sponsor of the bill, Charles Bennett, was at a time when the Soviet Union was clearly engaged in policies to dominate the world and destroy the freedoms we enjoy in the United States. Soviet policies included intentional anti-God and anti-Christian teachings and propaganda. It is instructive to read some of the comments by Charles Bennett made in support of his proposal on the floor of the House of Representatives:

"Nothing can be more certain than that our country was founded in a spiritual atmosphere and with a firm trust in God," Bennett proclaimed on the House Floor. "While the sentiment of trust in God is universal and timeless, these particular four words "In God We Trust" are indigenous to our country." Furthermore, Bennett invoked the cold war struggle in arguing for the measure. "In these days when imperialistic and materialistic communism seeks to attack and destroy freedom, we should continually look for ways to strengthen the foundations of our freedom," he said. Adding "In God We Trust" to currency, Bennett believed, would "serve as a constant reminder" that the nation's political and economic fortunes were tied to its spiritual faith.[11]

MY FATHER'S TESTIMONY: CHRIST IS THE ONLY HOPE

My father died on October 15, 2015. He was four days from turning ninety years old. In the months leading up to his passing, I visited him nearly every day. He had terminal cancer and was confined to a wheelchair, but his mind was clear and active to the day he passed away. He had plenty of time to reflect on his life and the things that mattered most.

Sometimes we discussed what I did that day, what was going on in the world, or the book he was reading. Other times we discussed the weather or what went on in his day that was positive or aggravating.

But at times we talked about deeper subjects. One day as we talked about the Bible and some of its meanings, he stopped for a moment, and then said quite deliberately, "I am convinced that Jesus Christ is the only hope in this world to save mankind."

I know that this statement came from his heart. I also sensed that his statement possessed more than one level of meaning. He felt the need to share that message with his son; both to ensure that he had passed his faith to the next generation, and to proclaim with his lips his faith in Jesus as Christ. We did not have many of these conversations when I was younger, and his demeanor led me to conclude he wanted to make sure he told me this before he passed on.

Knowing my father and his view of the world, I believe he intended an additional meaning. Without the love of Jesus Christ in the hearts of mankind, given the nature of man, we will ultimately destroy ourselves.

Jesus' teachings include repentance, forgiveness, and a love that includes your enemies. His actions while on earth, his willing self-sacrifice on a cross, and his resurrection collectively are unique. The very survival of humanity on earth requires the acceptance of the self-sacrificial love and principles given to us by Jesus Christ.

When I talk about societal morality guided and tempered by faith in God as essential to a free and thriving society, I must point out that mere faith in a god is not adequate. A worldwide survey of individuals ranked nations in order of how important religion was in their daily lives.[12] The ten nations ranked highest in percentage of citizens who consider religion important are all dominated or ruled by a faith other than Christian. All of them suffer from tyrannical rule or social chaos, widespread poverty, corruption, and a lack of personal freedoms and rights. Conversely, many societies that have been influenced by Christian faith rank among nations with the highest standard of living and personal freedom. Today several of those societies that benefited from Christian influence are drifting away from their Christian roots.

Indeed, if all persons in the world simply followed one sentence spoken by Jesus as recorded in the Bible in Matthew 7:12 (also found in Luke 6:31, NRSV), the need for armies, police, and most laws throughout the world would disappear. Just one sentence! Imagine if just one sentence could do that. What would happen if each of us went further and surrendered fully to the guidance of God's spirit through acceptance of Jesus as Emmanuel, Messiah, Christ.

My father taught me that one sentence from my earliest memories. As a youngster, I did not even know it came from the Bible. He taught it as a philosophy for how to live. I still hear him telling me, "Do unto others as you would have them do unto you."

OUR NATIONAL SOUL

We are a nation comprised of individuals. We are as strong as the combined strength of each individual citizen. We are and can continue to be the greatest nation on earth, but that requires unity. United in our understanding of what makes us great. United in our beliefs of what is right. United in our common purpose and who we see as our friends and enemies.

There used to be classes in public schools that taught the fundamentals of our nation's Constitution and other founding documents. There were ceremonies held on school grounds that imbued national pride and patriotism, respect for the flag, and gratitude for the sacrifices made by those in our military who sacrificed and died to gain and defend our freedoms.

These things I describe I regard as our nation's soul. I fear we are losing that soul. We seem to fail more and more to teach our children respect and pride in our nation. Political discord has devolved to the point where many in our legislative assemblies portray those across the aisle as the enemy, while real enemies and dangers to our freedoms operate with little recognition.

When Jesus talked about the house divided not being able to stand, he was talking about our souls. When we turn our fellow citizens into enemies, we are consciously following a course that compromises and sacrifices the very soul of our nation. The last time this happened over ten percent of men of fighting age in our nation lost their lives on Civil War battlefields. Today the world is too small and dangerous for us to survive another such division. Today the very soul of our nation is at stake. The society that forfeits its soul is doomed to destruction.

CHAPTER 2

A LACK OF UNDERSTANDING

"It is only when the people become ignorant and corrupt, when they degenerate into a populace, that they are incapable of exercising the sovereignty. Usurpation is then an easy attainment, and a usurper soon found. The people themselves become the willing instruments of their own debasement and ruin. Let us, then, look to the great cause, and endeavor to preserve it in full force. Let us by all wise and constitutional measures promote intelligence among the people as the best means of preserving our liberties."

James Monroe, First Inaugural Address, March 4, 1817

"They are darkened in their understanding, alienated from the life of God because of their ignorance and hardness of heart."

Ephesians 4:18, NRSV

"If a nation expects to be ignorant and free, in a state of civilization, it expects what never was and never will be."

Thomas Jefferson, January 6, 1816, letter to Charles Yancey

TO BAILOUT OR NOT TO BAILOUT?

President Obama stated in his first press conference after his election that he would do everything in his power when he gets into office to restore the economy. It is unfortunate that most Americans seem to think that the president of the United States is the person primarily responsible for making the economy prosper. In all times, but particularly in difficult economic times, voters base a significant part of their decision on who they pick for president upon the current state of the economy. The assumption that the president should be doing something significant for the economy, often interpreted as spending money somehow, is more likely to lead to greater economic problems, not economic recovery and prosperity.

Consider this, if the federal government is so powerful and influential in the economy that it can fix something like the economic situation in 2008 by simply borrowing and spending money, then why do we ever have economic downturns? If the economy is so easily manipulated, then why was everyone seemingly mystified about why the economy declines and what was to be done? Why was there such a debate about who and what and how to bailout? Obama and his supporters blamed President George Bush for "mishandling" the economy. In that case, the former president can share some blame for the magnitude of the problem, but the president merely recommends a budget to Congress.

It is Congress that is empowered by the Constitution to pass budgets, debt levels, and other legislation for the United States. Obama was a Senator for the previous four years. For two of those years, Congress was controlled by Republicans, and the other two were controlled by Democrats. Where were the legislation and spending bills that Congress passed that would provide the guidance and fix for the national economy that would have prevented the decline in the economy?

It appears such a fix was not in the possession of either of the two dominant political parties at the time. Indeed, the economic downturn can be explained in part resulting from excessive government spending prior to 2008. Why would we think that more government spending is going to fix the problem?

HEART OF THE PROBLEM

The heart of the economic recession of 2008 is found when we look into our nation's soul. The activities and actions that led to the financial crisis were brought about and enabled because individuals, banks, corporations, government-sponsored enterprises, and government officials, all acted in self-interest with no thought or regard for the long-term consequences of their actions. Drill down to each individual involved, and you will find they were either ignorant of the consequences of their actions, or they knew in their hearts that the activities they engaged in were wrong, but continued anyway.

We read in Ephesians (4:17-19 NRSV), "Now this I affirm and insist on in the Lord: you must no longer live as the Gentiles live, in the futility of their minds. They are darkened in their understanding, alienated from the life of God because of their ignorance and hardness of heart. They have lost all sensitivity and have abandoned themselves to licentiousness, greedy to practice every kind of impurity." Like the Gentiles referred to in the letter to the Ephesians, the multitude of people making financial decisions leading up to the 2008 crisis were either ignorant about what they were doing, or they chose to turn a blind eye to what their conscience told them was right and allowed greed to reign instead. This is what happens when we turn our eyes as individuals from the overarching guidance of God.

In general, economies flourish in spite of governments, not because of them. Do not get me wrong, some government regulation is required, but more is not necessarily better. It is not the role of government to create jobs and new wealth. It is the role of government to enable individuals to prosper and thrive in business by maintaining stability, security, and equitable regulations that provide consistency in transactions and prevent harmful business practices. The best governments perform this function with the least financial impact upon the individuals and businesses it serves.

Like the unseen hand of supply and demand that Adam Smith recognized as the guiding force in free-market economies, Christian morals and attitudes enable our free markets to function without the need for micromanaging regulation and overbearing enforcement that can stifle economic activity and growth. Businesses that follow moral principles in the conduct of their affairs, whether consciously or not, tend to fare better due to a higher degree of trust and customer satisfaction.[13]

BITING OUR HAND

A dangerous stance that is taken by many these days is that business is the enemy. This is biting our own hand. We are business. Businesses are who everyone works for. From sole proprietor businesses to partnerships to privately held corporations to large international conglomerates, they are all businesses. Except for individuals who work for the government, everyone else works for a business, and even the money for the wages of government employees would not be possible without businesses.

Government does have some useful regulatory functions that it performs, and at times there is a need to sanction individual businesses. Businesses can grow so large that they distort the market and stifle healthy competition resulting in the need for government intervention. Recently we have witnessed monopolistic tech and media companies selectively censoring individuals and businesses on what have become public communication platforms. This has led many government officials to recognize the need for intervention in such cases. But this should not lead us to the conclusion that businesses, in general, are inherently bad.

Another misunderstanding is the view of government as some separate entity. Ours is a government of, for, and by the people. We are the government. The government has authority, power, and functional ability only so long as citizens willingly support the government and obey its laws. This includes the provision of funding to government in the form of taxes.

I once heard it said by some commentators that lowering taxes is like stealing from the government. I was appalled to hear this. This is a point of view that was held in the past by supporters of the British crown at the time of the American Revolution. This is exactly the opposite of what our nation was founded upon. All funds come from the citizens. A reduction in taxes is not a gracious act by a benevolent government, but it represents a return to the citizens a portion of the funds that they relinquished for use toward the collective good of the nation.

A PRICE OF FREEDOM

In my view, there should be no mystery to the cause of economic downturns, and we have seen many such occurrences in our nation and the world before. Freedom has a price tag. One of the costs of freedom is the potential to fail. It is ironic that in this age of internet information providing an incredible depth of knowledge at our disposal, we are collectively so ignorant and seemingly helpless when our economic situation turns sour.

Ignorance seems to prevail from the voter on the street to our highest elected officials. We should not place all the blame for our problems upon the shoulders of elected officials because we as voters enabled them to gain their positions. The thing that concerns me most is the lack of understanding in the general public regarding our economic systems and how we can best manage them. Ignorance of the electorate is something that should be of great concern to anyone who loves freedom, prosperity, and all the other conveniences that our modern economy has brought us. As President Franklin Roosevelt stated, "There is nothing to fear but fear itself." I would restate this to say, "We have nothing to fear . . . but ignorance."

CHAPTER 3

RECESSION IN HISTORICAL PERSPECTIVE

"In history, a great volume is unrolled for our instruction, drawing the materials of future wisdom from the past errors and infirmities of mankind."

Edmund Burke, 1790

"Human nature will not change. In any future great national trial, compared with men of this, we shall have as weak and as strong, as silly and as wise, as bad and good. Let us therefore study the incidents in this as philosophy to learn wisdom from and none of them as wrongs to be avenged."

Abraham Lincoln, November 10, 1864

SOME HISTORICAL PERSPECTIVE is important for understanding how to move toward greater and continued prosperity. To get a full perspective, one needs to look at both the short-term past and longer-term history of our economy. When Obama took office in 2009, the media liked to compare the market crash of 2008 to that of 1929, and Obama was even compared to Franklin Roosevelt. There are similarities between the beliefs and actions of FDR and Obama, and things to learn by looking at what happened at that time. However, the media were not providing information or explanation. They were simply creating hype. Let us step back a bit and look at past events to develop a basis for moving forward in positive and constructive directions.

THE PANIC OF 1837

The decade prior to 1837 was a time of significant apparent economic growth. Land values soared, and prices for goods rose sharply, driven by speculative investment. Government spending rose for new construction projects, funded in part by borrowing from foreign investors. President Andrew Jackson opposed paper money and a central US bank. During his second term, Jackson joined with Congress to remove the charter for the 2nd Bank of the US.

As a result, on May 10, 1837, all banks stopped allowing individuals to exchange gold for paper currency. During the next six years, the nation was gripped by a depression with high unemployment. The bank deregulation spawned massive panic withdrawals that led to the failure of over forty percent of banks in the nation.[14]

GROWTH IN THE SECOND HALF OF THE 1800S AND THE PANIC OF 1893

After the Civil War, the economy grew significantly. The government enacted policies that encouraged the settlement of western lands and the development of natural resources. During this time, a slew of new innovations drove real gains in productivity and value-added products. These activities reflected increases in real net worth and lifestyle improvements. New innovations included the telephone, typewriter, phonograph, and light bulb.

By 1889, the US economy grew to become the largest in the world. Mining investment developed an abundance of metallic mines, particularly silver, whose production outpaced demand. In 1890, Congress passed several significant pieces of legislation, including the Sherman Act (a progressive anti-trust bill), the McKinley Tariff (a Republican protectionist bill), and the Sherman Silver Purchase Act (a Democrat metal market manipulation bill).

The tariff raised the rate for most imports to 48.4 percent, causing significant price increases. The Silver Act required the government to purchase silver to bolster the metal price and then use the silver as well as gold to back the US dollar. The Europeans required payment in gold only, which caused a depletion of US gold reserves. This depletion eroded confidence in the dollar.

The above items combined resulted in the panic of 1893. Bank runs spread widely, mines closed, and unemployment soared to as much as eighteen percent by 1894. Unemployment remained higher than normal for six years.

Interestingly, inflation before the panic resulted in part from the Republican-sponsored tariff, named for its principal sponsor, Senator William McKinley. Republicans were blamed for the high prices, and quite a few were voted out of office in 1892. Democrat Grover Cleveland was elected president in that year.

In the elections two and four years later, the Democrats were blamed for the panic of 1893 because they were the party in power, and were voted out in significant numbers. This resulted in the election of Republican McKinley as president in 1896, the former Senator whose bill helped exacerbate the recession.

I am not trying here to paint either political party in a positive or negative light. Focusing on party affiliation, rather than actual policy positions and past performance, may be misleading when entering the voting booth. Today, the focus on party politics rather than concrete positions and actions results in flawed, excessive, and wasteful activities and legislation. Most laws today are produced for political reasons, not sound financial or regulatory needs. The previous paragraphs show how deceptive party affiliation may be in your choice for an elected official.

Note during these difficult financial times, new businesses flourished. The bottom of a period of recession represents a time when new opportunities arise and existing enterprises that remain open to innovation and change may expand. Coca-Cola became a registered trademark in 1893. Dow Chemical was incorporated in 1897, and throughout the 1890s, Sears expanded from a relatively small enterprise into a 500-page catalog business.

THE PANIC OF 1907

Coming out of the panic of 1893, the country experienced a decade of economic growth. In 1901, an anarchist assassinated President McKinley, and Vice President Roosevelt took over as president. Roosevelt was a Republican, which at the time was the party that appealed most to so-called "Progressives."

Roosevelt, clearly a leader in this movement, attacked big business while defending labor unions. He railed against corrupt and illegal business practices and pushed for laws regulating businesses such as the Pure Food and Drug Act. He even proposed universal health care and national health insurance. He aggressively enforced the Sherman Act and caused more than forty monopolistic companies to be divided into smaller businesses. He stated his "Square Deal" policies were meant to benefit the middle class.

In July of 1906, the Hepburn Act established upper limits on railroad fares. This action caused railroad stocks to go down. Some of these stocks were collateral for borrowing to buy other stocks. The resulting run on institutions holding the notes collateralized with rail stocks led to the panic of 1907.

During the panic, J.P. Morgan voluntarily stepped in and brokered several deals with private businesses, the Secretary of the Treasury, and the president to prevent a complete collapse of the New York Stock Exchange. The losses on Wall Street created a contraction in the economy for the next year, and unemployment rose from three percent to about eight percent.

The financial "wizards" of Wall Street built a house of cards, linking borrowed money to stock values. A simple government action intended to help the "middle class" deal with high rail fares inadvertently pulled a card out of this house, causing the whole thing to collapse. This had a familiar ring to it one hundred years later in the so-called Great Recession of 2008.

THE CRASH OF 1929

The 1920s were another time of real expansion in the economy by the development of new technologies and expansion in productivity. By the end of the decade, the stock market came to be viewed by many as an endless wealth generator. Market hype included some fraudulent stock promotions and encouraged leveraged stock purchases using borrowed money. Investment trusts typically valued at greater than the sum of their stock portfolios also became common.

Many experts have studied why the 1929 crash occurred. I think it was a combination of things. The market peaked on September 3 with a DJIA of 381.17. The market began its well-known dive on October 24, and by the end of October 29, the DJIA was at 230.07, a loss of forty percent from the high in September.

The loss in perceived wealth and real savings resulted in a significant slowing in the economy over the next several months. Industrial production fell by eleven percent, and unemployment rose from three to eight percent. The DJIA seemed to stabilize early in 1930, but began a precipitous two-year slide until it bottomed out in June of 1932 at a value of 41.22.

During the 1930s, the federal government took steps, under both Hoover and Roosevelt, in sincere efforts to aid the economic condition. Some were helpful, while others were filled with unintended consequences that made problems worse. Consider the following partial listing of events in the first half of the decade:

1930 The Smoot-Hawley Tariff Act raised tariffs by over 50% on over 20,000 items. This resulted in retaliations from other governments that raised prices and restricted trade activity.

1932 The Emergency Relief and Construction Act created, among other things, the Reconstruction Finance Corporation, which provided two billion dollars in aid to states and local governments and loans to select private businesses. It also regulated industry to the point where government told private enterprises how to run their business. Although begun under Hoover, and criticized by Roosevelt in his election campaign for excessive spending, Roosevelt's New Deal continued the program and created additional spending regulations.

1932 The Norris-LaGuardia Act strengthened the ability of unions to organize.

1932 Income tax rates were increased to roughly double the personal income tax rate most people paid and increased the upper marginal rate from twenty-five to sixty-three percent.

1930–1933 The Federal Reserve used traditional money supply metrics, which led them to take no action to ease the money supply and avert panic bank runs, causing massive bank failures. Milton Friedman stated that the failure of the Federal Reserve to maintain the money supply was the prime reason the recession of the early 1930s grew in severity and extended time to become the Great Depression.[15]

1933 New Deal Legislation included NIRA, parts of which were found to be unconstitutional in 1935. NIRA included sweeping regulations that protected union bargaining rights, regulated industries, allowed cartels and monopolies, set price floors, and established the Public Works Administration. The Act created the National Recovery Administration (NRA) that produced thousands of pages of regulations. Under the Act, a massive wave of union organization began. Also, price-fixing was undertaken to try to combat deflation.

1933 The Banking Act created the FDIC with regulations and deposit insurance that served to stabilize the banking industry.

1934 A severe drought in the Midwest created dust bowl

conditions that uprooted thousands of farmers. This led Congress to pass the Soil Conservation Act in 1935.

1935 The National Labor Relations Act prevented employers from interfering with union organization and required employers to bargain collectively with union representatives. It also created the National Labor Relations Board.

1935 The Revenue Act of 1935 raised income tax rates for all incomes above $50,000 and the marginal upper rate to seventy-nine percent. It also increased rates on corporations, estates, and gifts.

1935 The Social Security Act created the Social Security Administration and established the Social Security Tax. This law was challenged in court and was initially found unconstitutional but later was upheld, citing that it was in the interest of the general welfare of the nation. The payroll withholding tax went into effect in 1937.

1935 Creation of the Works Projects Administration funded various public works projects devised to create temporary jobs.

From 1930 to 1936 the federal budget more than doubled from four billion to 9.2 billion dollars and from a surplus of 0.9 billion dollars to a deficit of four billion dollars. This 2.5-fold increase in the budget and swing to borrowing four percent of GDP occurred when the economy was suffering from a severe contraction in the money supply. At the same time, tax rates doubled for most individuals, and more than tripled for higher income tax brackets.

In 1937 the nation experienced a second recession likely brought about in part by Federal Reserve increases in bank reserves and US Treasury policy of gold sterilization.[16] Also Social Security taxes began to be collected. All these siphoned money from the cash-strapped economy. This, combined with a business community wary of what else the government might do, caused the second greatest economic contraction in the century.

This could have been a typical recession like the ones discussed previously. During the 1932 election, Roosevelt blamed Hoover for the poor economic conditions. The criticisms included several of Hoover's policies later adopted by Roosevelt under different names. Political rhetoric confuses the actual cause and effects of this period. Liberal thinkers attribute all that Roosevelt did to the rise in GDP once Roosevelt took office, while Republicans see little value in anything that Roosevelt did and cite double-digit unemployment continuing until we entered World War II. Both are partially right, and partially wrong.

Congress is charged with the regulation of commerce. Regulation creates rules of conduct to provide for smooth and stable transactions within the economy, both from state to state and between states and other nations. Congress did devise some regulations during the 1930s that were of significant benefit for the economy. Congress relaxed, modified, or removed some of those laws in more recent years to our detriment. On the other hand, other regulations directly manipulated prices and businesses, working against competitive market forces that enable economies to adjust, grow, and create new employment opportunities.

New Deal legislation and Supreme Court rulings that found Social Security and certain other Congressional actions constitutional erased the line separating what is and is not appropriate for federal government regulation and spending. Some government programs constructed electric generation facilities and other useful public works. However, other spending projects simply made work for individuals that did not result in useful, productive output. Doing this with borrowed money diminishes the economy.

Borrowing money to give someone a job without creating enterprise by which that person can be employed the following year, merely creates debt with no way to pay it back. We have yet to pay back money borrowed in the 1930s.

RECESSION OF 1980-1982

On the day before Thanksgiving in November 1982, I received notice I was being laid off from my job together with over 90% of the exploration staff of Texasgulf, Inc. The company that two years earlier ranked among the 200 most profitable corporations in the US, was now a subsidiary of a foreign conglomerate, and suffering sizeable losses.

That month marked the highest unemployment rate experienced in the United States between the end of the Great Depression in 1940, and the radical reaction to COVID-19 in April 2020. Despite the hype over the period beginning in 2008 now referred to as the Great Recession, the peak unemployment rate in 2009 was slightly less than in 1982.

To understand the conditions of 1982, we go back to the 1960s when the United States engaged in "wars" both foreign and domestic. In 1964 the Johnson administration declared war on poverty. At the same time, the US had thousands of military advisors on the ground in Vietnam, and American warplanes began bombardment operations to support the South Vietnamese military. The following year American ground troops landed in Da Nang, beginning our direct involvement in the war that officially continued until 1973.

That same year the Arab members of the Organization of Oil Exporting Countries (OPEC) imposed an embargo on oil exports to the United States. To fight inflation and unemployment, President Nixon took the dollar off the gold standard and imposed increased tariffs that hurt OPEC nations. When the United States provided aid to Israel in the Arab-Israeli war, OPEC responded with the embargo. Oil prices quadrupled before easing somewhat but never returned to pre-embargo prices.

Prices for energy, as well as most industrial production in the US, also increased due to the rise of environmentalism in the 1970s. This led to early 1970s restrictions on oil facilities expansion and raised the cost of oil production. The combination of increased spending on "wars" and the shock of sharply increased energy prices, resulted in persistent escalating inflation rates. The anticipation of inflation by government, employees, producers, and businesses resulted in a vicious circle of wage and price escalation. Efforts by the Nixon and later administrations to curb inflation with wage and price controls merely resulted in hampering businesses, who were left with no options but to lay-off employees to curb costs.

All these factors led to a stagnation of productivity growth, resulting in persistent moderately high unemployment. The simultaneous conditions of inflation and economic stagnation led to the creation of the new term, stagflation.

In 1979, with no clear options remaining to fight the economic malaise facing the nation, President Carter nominated Paul Volker as chairman of the Federal Reserve. Volker entered the position with the expressed intention of bringing inflation under control. The Fed quickly moved under his leadership to restrict the money supply. A sharp increase in interest rates led to the 1980–1982 recession.

Jimmy Carter lost his bid for re-election in 1980 primarily due to the state of the economy. Carter's successor, Ronald Reagan, continued the Federal Reserve policies, and ran for re-election under the slogan "Stay the Course." The course he continued was started under the Carter Administration. I heard commentary recently about the Fed policy being lauded for bringing inflation under control. The discussion gave credit to Paul Volker and Ronald Reagan. No mention was made of the president that started the praiseworthy course of action.

Under Volcker, the Fed kept interest rates high until October 1982, when inflation hit a low of five percent. Interest rates were then allowed to fall, quickly spurring growth in the economy.[17] From that time until 2001, controlling spending to bring the deficit under control became a policy that Congress pursued.[18] The level of resolve of lawmakers and their success in such efforts varied, but by the end of the 1990s a balanced budget was achieved.

Today former President Bill Clinton often receives credit for that achievement, but in reality, it was Republicans in Congress that held the line on increases in spending proposed by Clinton. The resolve of a Republican Congress in the 1990s resulted in controlling spending in the same way the resolve of a Democrat appointed Fed-Chairman brought inflation under control in the 1980s.

CHAPTER 4

THE KEY TO THE SUCCESS OF THE UNITED STATES OF AMERICA

"Those who expect to reap the blessings of freedom must, like men, undergo the fatigue of supporting it."

Thomas Paine, 1777

"I would rather be exposed to the inconveniences attending too much liberty than to those attending too small a degree of it."

Thomas Jefferson, 1791

"A free, virtuous, and enlightened people know well the great principles and causes on which their happiness depends, ..."

James Monroe, November 14, 1820

AMERICAN SUCCESS

The United States of America is one of the most economically successful nations the world has seen. In the first one hundred years of our existence, the nation grew from a collection of thirteen colonies clinging to the Atlantic coast to a nation that spanned across the continent of North America. At the time of our founding, the US gross domestic product (GDP) paled in comparison to the economic powers of the time in China, India, and Europe. Our very existence appeared tenuous. Despite the attempt by Great Britain in 1812 to reassert its control over the infant nation, and despite the soul-wrenching Civil War in the 1860s, the US GDP grew 8,291 percent from 1789 to 1890.[19] In our first official year as a nation, the size of our economy was only five percent the size of the world's largest economy in China. By 1890, the United States surpassed China as the largest economy on the planet.[20]

For the next 125 years, we remained the largest economy in the world. In recent years China reasserted itself as a dominant economic power on the international stage, and has overtaken the US in total GDP, adjusted for variations in the purchasing power between nations Purchasing Power Parity (PPP). Hereinafter GDP adjusted for PPP will be referred to as GDP4.[21] The size of the Chinese GDP4 is understandable considering they have nearly five times the population of the United States, but these absolute numbers do not reflect the individual living standards of the inhabitants of each nation.[22]

To consider how citizens of one nation fare economically relative to another nation, we look at GDP4 per capita.[23] According to World Bank statistics for the year 2019, the per capita GDP4 for China and the United States were $16,785 and $65,118, respectively. Thus, we see the per capita GDP4 of the US is nearly four times that of China. Broaden the comparison to the fourteen nations with more than one hundred million inhabitants, and the United States still retains the highest GDP4 by considerable margins.

When compared to all nations in 2019, according to World Bank data, the United States ranks ahead of all but seven countries and two autonomous protectorates. Note that all nine of these entities have populations less than ten million.[24] All nine also benefit from one or more of the following advantages:

- Presence of a large oil resource within their territory.
- Historical protected and privileged status maintained by one or more larger nations.
- Small homogenous population with an extended history of shared stable heritage that enabled development of financial and technical niches.

When leveraged relative to their populations, the advantages result in exceptional per capita incomes. We can learn lessons from some of these nations, particularly those of the third category. Fundamentally, the lessons demonstrate they organize to take the best advantage of free-market capitalism, and educate citizens to appreciate their nation and become productive contributing members of society.

Some experts point out that per capita GDP data does not reflect income inequality, and that the United States rates poorly when considering the separation between rich and poor. This argument ignores the fact that the United States starts with a relatively high bar for upper-income individuals. Of the ten wealthiest individuals in the world, eight of them live in the United States.[25]

There may be a greater separation between the top five percent and bottom five percent, but that is because the top is higher than other countries. The poorest 10% in the US are better off economically than 70% of the remaining world's population.[26] In terms of quality of life, the poor in our nation rank better than those in Germany, Japan, or France, and better than the top 10% of people in places such as Portugal, Russia, or Mexico.

Beyond the gross domestic product numbers, we see the success of the United States in other ways as well. All the nations mentioned having high per capita GDP4 benefit from the defense umbrella the United States maintained over Europe, the Middle East, and Asia since World War II. This benefit comes at considerable expense to the American taxpayers, and the lives of young American soldiers. Many nations, including former enemies such as Japan and China, owe much of their development to innovations and technologies acquired from the US.

Looking at another aspect, United States citizens contribute to charitable causes at a higher rate than all other nations. We give to charities two times more than the next highest nation New Zealand. We give considerably more than all nations ranked higher in per capita GDP than the US, including more than ten times that of Norway and Switzerland.[27] If we took the difference in giving between the US and Switzerland and assumed in the last forty years it had been invested in growing our GDP, in theory, we could have generated a per capita GDP equivalent or greater than Singapore.[28] Despite all the faults some find with America, the world has benefited greatly from our nation.

The preceding statistics are not intended to diminish or justify the disparities that our poorer citizens experience, but rather show how successful we have been collectively as a nation. A concern of this book is that we are not doing as well as we could, due in large part to losing sight as a society of the principles and values that led to our great success. Disparities in our nation do exist that I believe we need to address. We should not allow successes to blind us to the plight of those on the low end of the income scale.

FREEDOM

There is one distinctively American characteristic key to our success—individual freedom. The fierce demand for and protection of individual freedoms by our founders was no accident, but rather the result of purposeful and intentional deliberations and action on their part. To emphasize the importance of protecting individual freedoms, Congress passed a bill in less than seven months from the start of its first session in 1789 containing the first ten amendments to the Constitution.

Americans have been characterized by their independent individualistic thought. Those holding political office were not there to hand out privileges or patronage, but to serve the public's best interests through sound fiscal management and well-reasoned and necessary legislation, passed within the narrow confines of the Constitution.

A free society is reliant on the strength of character and conviction of each citizen. We rely on each citizen to do the right thing. As the overall reliability of individuals declines, the need for a heavier hand in the form of centralized government control increases. When individuals are properly socialized by loving parents to be high-quality citizens, we do not require the constant addition of formal laws and regulations. As laws, regulations, and requirements increase, freedom declines. With increase in regulation and bureaucracy also comes the greater possibility of abuses in government.

Thus, with freedom comes responsibility on the part of each citizen. The primary responsibility for the provision of food, shelter, clothing, health care, education, personal transportation, and other necessities of life lies directly upon each individual adult citizen, not upon the national treasury. The legislative and executive representatives at every level in our nation have a duty to the American taxpayers that tax money will be spent appropriately and wisely. Furthermore, governmental financial responsibilities were originally, and always intended to be, limited.

TRADING FREEDOM FOR MORE GOVERNMENT

In the last ninety years, the federal government expanded significantly into social programs such as education, health insurance, home loans, and retirement. Prior to the 1930s, military defense of the nation accounted on average for about seventy percent of all federal spending.[29] This included veterans' benefits and interest on debt incurred for military expenses. Essentially, during the first 140 years of the nation, we only incurred debt to finance defense spending and paid those debts down during times of peace. For over 100 years, the federal government operated without corporate and personal income taxes.

In 2019 taxation and social spending programs, including Social Security, accounted for seventy-four percent of federal expenditures, while defense spending represented about twenty-six percent.[30] The level of defense versus domestic spending reversed from what it was for the first half of our nation's history. Budget deficits and interest result from both types of spending, regardless of times of war or peace.

In the last ninety years the federal government expanded into social programs that rightfully are the responsibility of the individual, employers, or individual states. Contrary to the notion that this move represents compassionate and socially responsible governance, it can be argued that much of this represents a lack of fiscal restraint and promotion of social irresponsibility.

This promotion has grown the entire society's propensity to encumber ourselves with considerable personal and public debt. Even individuals who remain debt free are encumbered by irresponsible government bureaucrats, legislators, and executives, who have piled enormous public debts on national and state levels. As we become more reliant on government to solve our problems and meet our needs and wants, the pressure on governments to supply those wants and needs by incurring more debt increases.

Incurring debt reduces freedom. The greater the debt, the less your freedom. The staggering debt levels of the United States places all of us in a precarious position where all it may take is one crisis that starts a domino effect to bring about the economic demise of our nation. I am afraid too many Americans cannot conceive of such a threat. But with each passing day, and more and more debt being added, with no plan for reversing this trend, we draw closer to losing the freedoms and standard of living that we presently enjoy.

Overburdening debt even threatens our national security. The greatest strength of the United States is not in our military, but in our financial and industrial production capacities. Too much debt causing the dollar to become discredited in world markets could render our government unable to afford to operate our military planes and equipment or pay the wages of our military personnel. Such changes in national fortunes can occur rapidly.

In 1913 Germany was one of the major economic powerhouses in the world. Few would have thought that ten years in the future, Germany would be economically devastated. In the 1928 US elections, few gave thought to the possibility that economies worldwide would suffer widespread unemployment and poverty. But in three years from 1929 to 1932, unemployment in the United States went from three percent to more than twenty-three percent.

In the 1980s the Soviet Union collapsed because of Western economic policies that resulted in near bankruptcy of the Russian economy, and the fall of the "Iron Curtain." In the economic conditions of the spring of 2019, if the United States does nothing, Chinese and Russian economic policies could potentially result in a similar economic collapse of the United States.

A nation does considerable disservice to its citizens when it takes upon itself the responsibility for provision of personal needs that have historically and rightly been the fruits of an individual's livelihood. By doing so, the government absolves the individual of responsibility for personal provision of necessities, diminishing the independence and strength of the individual. A nation is only as strong as the collective sum of its individuals. A nation of individuals thus weakened does itself become weaker. We are training ourselves to become a third-world nation of helpless sheep.

CHAPTER 5

A NATION OF SHEEP

"In the end, more than they wanted freedom, they wanted security. They wanted a comfortable life, and they lost it all—security, comfort, and freedom. When . . . the freedom they wished for was freedom from responsibility, then Athens ceased to be free."

Sir Edward Gibbon, 1776

"Society will develop a new kind of servitude which covers the surface of society with a network of complicated rules, through which the most original minds and the most energetic characters cannot penetrate. It does not tyrannise, but it compresses, enervates, extinguishes, and stupefies a people, till each nation is reduced to nothing better than a flock of timid and industrious animals, of which the government is the shepherd."

Alexis de Tocqueville, 1835

FLYING SHEEP

I fear we are becoming a nation of sheep. When something goes wrong, we collectively look to our government to save us from whatever the problem may be. Our nation has risen to the level of prosperity we presently enjoy because each of us is free to pursue our dreams. Most of us fail to take full advantage of this freedom, but enough of us have in the past to result in a sustained display of ingenuity and invention that is unprecedented in human history. Yet today, when faced with problems in our society, instead of just getting up and doing something about it, we turn to our government representatives for a solution. We do this as if the problem will magically go away by adding another convoluted law to the incredibly complex volumes already compiled. The response by and to the airline industry after 9/11 is an example.

The airline industry in the United States is a private commercial enterprise. Perhaps I am naïve, but in the days after September 11, 2001, I thought that a forward-thinking commercial airline executive would step up and initiate their own stringent baggage checking system, place guards on all their airliners, and advertise, "You can fly safely with our airline!"

This did not happen. Instead, every airline lay down, gave up, and cried to the government for help. Where is the "can-do" American spirit and ingenuity? Was government regulation already so strong that the private businesses involved were unable to respond on their own without permission from the government? I don't know the answer to this, but if it's "yes," then the regulations were already doing more harm than good.

The first action taken by Congress was to provide billions of dollars in assistance to the airline industry. I can understand some assistance to compensate for the government-ordered closing of airports immediately following September 11, but we should remember this is a private enterprise. The loss of business for the airlines over the longer term was a public relations problem they needed to overcome. I have already given the approach I would have taken. They had options. From the perspective of Congress, our elected officials should have looked at the larger picture. If the airline industry is shrinking, then the money that would be spent there is going to go somewhere else. If airline ticket sales decline, that is not the end of the world for our nation collectively, but it just means economic opportunities for other industries.

Note that retail sales, led by car sales, soared in October following September 11. Apparently, some Americans came up with their own solution to terrorists on airliners: They would drive instead, or stay home and fix up their house.

Some may think I am crazy to suggest this, but flying on commercial airlines actually became safer on September 11, 2001. The greatest step taken to avert another World Trade Center type disaster was not taken in the months and years that followed, with the creation of another federal government department; it was taken the same day on September 11, 2001. When the passengers on UA Flight 93 that crashed into Pennsylvania stood up and attempted to regain control of that airplane, they demonstrated what would happen if another such attempt was made on an airliner carrying able-bodied Americans. They stopped being sheep and started being Americans.

Armed with the knowledge of September 11, it's unlikely that Americans riding in a commercial airliner will let their aircraft be commandeered and used as a terrorist bomb. This fact has probably done more to protect against another September 11 type attack than anything the government has done or will do in the future.

We have squandered billions of dollars in the name of homeland security when the reality is this is the best outcome terrorists could hope for. In the name of making ourselves secure, we will destroy ourselves by allowing our politicians to spend billions, or now trillions, on things that are of little or no worth, while trying to appear as if they are doing something about the problem of the day.

POLITICAL COURAGE VS SHEEP

It can be a heady experience for an elected representative to have constituents come to him or her and ask for assistance in solving their problems. It is easy, particularly in the emotional atmospheres surrounding the aftermath of events such as September 11, to say "Yes" to such requests and open the pocketbooks of the taxpayers. It is much more difficult to say, "No, you need to solve this problem on your own." We need elected officials that have such courage, the courage to tell their constituents to stop acting like sheep and stand up tall and act like Americans.

When the financial crisis of 2008 hit home for investment bankers and automakers, most of them lined up to take handouts from the federal government, at the expense of the American taxpayer. Our representatives in Congress incredibly voted to hand out hundreds of billions of dollars for such programs as the Troubled Asset Relief Program (TARP) and the American Recovery and Reinvestment Act (ARRA), much of which carried little oversight or accountability. Indeed, the accountability of ARRA spending was designed not to ensure that it would be spent appropriately or beneficially, but so that politicians could show how many "jobs" were "saved or created." Artificial accounting requirements increased the cost of performing the work being funded, which reduced the potential economic benefit of the spending.

From what I saw first-hand working for a construction company during that time, most of the spending did not create new jobs, but displaced losses of state revenue. Much of the spending also went to projects of dubious necessity. The recordkeeping requirements and new bureaucracies created to track the Congress-imposed paperwork made this spending more costly and thus less efficient. The overall net effect of such stimulus money is a net loss of jobs. Unfortunately, the cumulative effect is difficult to determine, because there are many other factors that are constantly at work, both adding and decreasing jobs.

FREEDOM OR TYRANNY?

Our nation is great because our citizens are free to pursue their dreams. Our love, pursuit, and defense of freedom at home and around the world is the one great distinguishing characteristic of Americans. Thomas Jefferson once said, "The price of freedom is eternal vigilance." This truth applies to our political and economic arenas, as well as on battlefields.

It apparently never occurred to present-day Americans that a free marketplace can provide a much swifter and stronger response for airline security or economic recessions than anything the federal government may devise. There are many nations in this world whose populations are easily manipulated by ruling tyrants. Citizens of such nations perceive little hope of influencing the actions of the government, and thus are resigned to accept whatever fate befalls them. They are completely at the whim and mercy of their leader. They are to their leader like a herd of sheep.

Our nation's founders fought the American Revolution because the colonists were proud men not to be patronized, abused, and herded, like so many cattle or sheep, property of the king. When they finally won their freedom, many at great sacrifice, they strove to establish a form of governance that would not allow the government to become too overbearing or subject to abuse by those who would seek to be overlords. The founding fathers studied history and purposefully cast out European thinking and approaches to governance.

As we lean more and more upon our government to become involved in our lives, we slowly but steadily relinquish the freedom that our ancestors and our present military personnel have paid so dearly to acquire and maintain. For the most part, those who ask for some new regulation are well intentioned, but good intentions abound throughout the follies of history. When we seek a solution, we should first look to ourselves. Can we solve this one on our own? Then if we must involve the government, we should seek a solution that ensures the preservation of the greatest degree of freedom.

Sheep want to be herded and looked after. Americans, real Americans, want to be free, free to pursue their dreams. Are we going to preserve the American dream of freedom, or become a dismal third-world nation of sheep? You decide.

CHAPTER 6

PARTY POLITICS

"There is nothing I dread so much as the division of the republic into two great parties, each arranged under its leader, and concerting measures in opposition to each other. This, in my humble apprehension, is to be dreaded as the greatest political evil under our constitution."

John Adams, October 2, 1780

"If a political party does not have its foundation in the determination to advance a cause that is right and that is moral, then it is not a political party; it is merely a conspiracy to seize power."

Dwight D. Eisenhower, March 6, 1956

"The alternate domination of one faction over another, sharpened by the spirit of revenge, natural to party dissension, which in different ages and countries has perpetrated the most horrid enormities, is itself a frightful despotism. But this leads at length to a more formal and permanent despotism. The disorders and miseries, which result, gradually incline the minds of men to seek security and repose in the absolute power of an individual; and sooner or later the chief of some prevailing faction, more able or more fortunate than his competitors, turns this disposition to the purposes of his own elevation, on the ruins of public liberty."

George Washington, Farewell Address, 1796

THE UNDIVIDED

In the small part of the nation that I live in, there is not great division. I get up during the week, go to work, and endeavor with my coworkers to acquire, build, and complete quality construction projects in a safe and timely manner. We are united in our efforts and commitment to our goal.

Despite the inconveniences that construction can impose at times upon adjacent residents, for the most part, I find neighboring citizens receptive and reasonable when informed about our projects with patience and understanding. Although, at times, we may consider some of the restrictions imposed by government agencies to go beyond reason, we can usually work out and resolve local regulatory issues with time and meetings that enable each party to understand the limitations and intentions of the others. We also must compete against other contractors in both private and public bids, and yet our relationships with individuals in competing companies are, for the most part, congenial and respectful.

I go home, and my wife and I are united in our hopes and desires for our children's success and contentment. There may not always be harmony in all the relationships within our extended families, but we are still bound by a common hope for our loved ones.

I greet my neighbors next door and down the street. We're all different in many ways. We differ in philosophical, religious, cultural, and political beliefs; but we all have in common our concerns, dreams, and desires for our families, and the safety of our neighborhood. I walk to the park and see children, parents, grandchildren, and grandparents, playing or just relaxing, enjoying the day. Playground, basketball, baseball, soccer, volleyball, dogs retrieving, kites flying, birthday parties, swimming in the summertime. People from different backgrounds, occupations, races, parts of the country, different nations. Always, I can greet them, and they return a smile and hello. Rarely do I encounter negativity and never conflict.

I go to church on Sunday mornings and other times during the week, and we're united in our determination to impart upon ourselves, and share with others, the love God teaches us through his son, Jesus Christ. We may not always agree on every point of doctrine, or course of ministry, but we are of the same mind in Christ.

EXTREME DIVIDE

The great division within our nation is not on the level of my daily life. I suspect this is the same with most people. The great division is external to our daily lives. We learn of the division from news reports; the television, radio, internet, podcasts, however one informs themselves.

The divide is caused by extreme views which have forced themselves to the center of political platforms. Special interests that push beyond the level of equality to special guarded politically correct treatment enforced by like-minded individuals, combined with complicit judges and media.

Such extremism has now infected the dominant political party in our nation. We were warned by George Washington, more than two hundred years ago, of the danger of the potential hijacking of a political party by a particular faction to gain power, "on the ruins of public liberty." It is now coming to pass. By October 2019, the leaders of the House of Representatives appeared consumed and focused entirely on party vengeance. Without regard to the disastrous precedents they are setting for the future, they proceeded on innuendo and fabricated scenarios.

Further, around the country judges, prosecutors, and legislatures all endeavor to block attempts by the executive branch to enforce federal laws. They subpoena personal tax and other records of the sitting president, and seek to change election laws—all targeted specifically at former President Donald Trump. This unrelenting barrage of attacks is unprecedented, and if sustained establishes a near-impossible set of circumstances for future presidents. At the same time, colleagues within their Democrat Party propose policies and programs with price-tags that reach well beyond the existing tax base at a time when spending is already out of control.

Party politics degenerated to the point where partisan operatives within the bureaucracy worked to counter and undermine the policies of the prevailing administration. This truly creates a house divided against itself, and compromises the electoral process. Individual voters will conclude their vote is meaningless, because it can be canceled out by a minority of well-placed unelected bureaucrats in Washington, DC.

Fueling and fanning the flames of these dangerous proceedings and proposals are an unquestioning media who appear to be complicit in the extremist views. These actions and views are in direct conflict with reasoned political discourse, sound fiscal policy, and the Constitution's concise wording and original intent. Our Founders sought as best as they could to create a governing document that would serve to protect hard-won freedoms, but they also warned us that those freedoms were fragile and would require constant effort to keep.

Seeking out the truth, at a time when those considered to be responsible for doing so merely let the politicians speak without questioning their voracity, is somewhere between difficult and impossible. We need to have the courage to call out the politicians and complicit media when their rhetoric crosses the line from truth to falsehood, and their actions cross the line from reason to outlandish and vindictive. Failure to do so will just as surely doom our nation to disaster as that of overwhelming violence from a foreign power.

SELF-EVIDENT TRUTHS

There are fundamental ideas and values that should not be portrayed as the sole possession of one party or another. Basic principles that form the basis for a sound and secure nation should be supported by all in elected public office. I view protection of the freedoms and rights of individual citizens, and sound fiscal management of public funds, as the two most important principles.

Freedoms and rights cover a broad spectrum of concepts that are fundamental to what America stands for. The list of specific items that one or the other party holds up against another grows wearily long. I could list several commonly tossed about to disparage opponents, often unjustly, but I provide here just two examples that bother me: patriotism and racism.

Republicans often will accuse Democrats of not being patriotic, lacking a sincere concern for their nation merely because they choose to identify as a Democrat. This unfairly labels many Democrats who have a sincere concern for this nation, but differ in their perspective of how best to administer it. On the other hand, some Democrats routinely categorically call Republicans racist. This label unjustly defies the truth that Republicans support racial equality, and clouds the reality of the racist past and present of the Democratic Party.

Following the November 2020 election, some Democratic Congressional candidates who lost their election complained that Republicans had unfairly portrayed all Democrats as being in favor of defunding the police. Those individuals claimed that they had always supported the police and what the Republicans did was unfair. They fail to recognize the irony of their complaint, ignoring that they for years have portrayed all Republicans to be bigoted racists, and uncaring of the poor and children. Both characterizations are false, but I believe the latter has been a much more egregious and prolonged falsehood.

False generalizations of opposing parties fuel the vast divide that cripples reasoned discourse. We must hold politicians accountable for distortions and false statements made in efforts to gain, hold, and wield power. The American people need to recognize and understand the presence and destructive nature of the lies in political rhetoric.

CHAPTER 7

THE LIE OF THE RHETORIC

"There is no nation on earth powerful enough to accomplish our overthrow . . . . Our destruction, should it come at all, will be from another quarter. From the inattention of the people to the concerns of their government, from their carelessness and negligence, I must confess that I do apprehend some danger. I fear that they may place too implicit a confidence in their public servants, and fail properly to scrutinize their conduct; that in this way they may be made the dupes of designing men, and become the instruments of their own undoing."

Daniel Webster, June 1, 1837

EXAMPLES

The term capitalism is today generally placed as an end member opposite socialism or communism. This belies a complete misunderstanding of economics as presented by Adam Smith. His writings were an observation of how real economies work. Having this understanding can help to maximize the efficiency of markets, and perhaps guide useful regulations of economic systems.

Karl Marx's writings, on the other hand, are disconnected from reality. His was a vision of how he thought the world should be, not how it really is. He wove his vision into a prediction of the future that did not actually come true, and he had no practical explanation of how to get there. Communism has no use as an economic system because it does not actually describe the real-world practice of how it is to be employed. Karl Marx promoted the term *capitalism* in a negative way, to create an evil opposite of the imagined Utopia he was envisioning. His arguments were based upon his personal interpretations of current events of his time, heavily tainted by his radical political persuasions that he attempted to paint with his rhetoric.

His Communist Manifesto proposes to abolish private property and rights of inheritance, and centralize all credit, means of communication, transportation, and industrial and agricultural production in the hands of the state. He implies the state would organize where and how you may live. He states that, "their ends can be attained only by the forcible overthrow of all existing social conditions."[31]

Socialism is a choice that nations make with respect to the government becoming an active participant in the marketplace. Some believe that the government can more equitably distribute the wealth generated from their markets. Others believe that free markets are too fraught with inefficiencies and disruptive up and down cycles that they perceive to be undesirable. These beliefs are unfortunate, unfounded, and are propagated largely by political rhetoric. Capitalism (free markets) is how economies work. Socialism is how governments meddle with economies.

Some developed nations decide as a society to provide specific benefits to all citizens equally. Medical care is a common cost certain societies choose to collectively share via government administration. Many in our nation have pointed to such countries as examples of what we should emulate. It is important to remember when considering this that the United States collectively has developed the most advanced medical technology by having a system that greatly rewards medical innovation. Enabled and encouraged by free-market economics, American medical technology has saved and enhanced countless lives throughout the world.

Beyond creating market inefficiencies, embracing socialism gives increasing power to a centralized government. The greater that power, the more susceptible it becomes to dominance by factions or individuals. Socialism is a path tyrants often take toward fascism and communism.

Modern political economics, developed and taught to our present generation, speaks of mixed economies where government moderates the private marketplace to create a stable growing economy. This viewpoint has degenerated into a view of private business as some beast requiring caging and controlling, and government as the great tamer and savior of the economy. This gives too much credit to government and leads to the view by many that all pursuits of government are good and beneficial, and private business is evil and corrupt.

I have been told by some that medical care is too large and complex to be trusted to the free market. This, they claim, is justification for the federal government to create a unified one-payer government health care system. This flies contrary to all we know about government programs and free markets.

One of the largest and most efficient product distribution systems in the world is the provision of food in the United States. Food is clearly a more vital fundamental necessity to human existence than medical care. The variety and abundance of food available in the United States is completely taken for granted by Americans. Average Americans have absolutely no appreciation for the vast array of foods at their ready disposal. In many cities, this array is available twenty-four hours per day, seven days per week.

We have foods available from all over the planet. What we have for food in this nation today in scale, quality, and availability to every citizen, is unmatched in the history of the world. Yet it is all performed with little or no coordination by the government. All the food in our supermarkets and restaurants is grown, transported, prepared, and distributed by private free enterprises. The government performs marginally in trade regulations, safety inspections, and funding to welfare recipients.

How is it possible that such a vast global distribution system is so successful and efficient and yet not run by the government? It's possible because the reality is that a free market is the most efficient organizational method for an economy. Consumers dictate to producers what they want by what they consume. This basic principle, the law of supply and demand, was understood since the time of the birth of our nation. Yet, we have failed to educate ourselves and our children in this regard. It would appear even many in Congress don't understand this.

As a nation, for some reason, we think economic problems are the fault of private business that need to be solved by government. This is why so many in our nation think that we need to have health care run by government, while we have private companies in a free market providing us the most basic necessity of food, and we think nothing of it.

One big reason why we have come to this point is that there is confusion when considering the past. Some look at things that happened and interpret it as capitalism gone bad when it was not capitalism, but a perversion of the markets by government.

Going back to medical care, many individuals think the medical care system was broken in the private sector and needed fixing by the federal government. This ignores the fact that most medical care is already provided by government funding. The heavy government involvement in medical care badly skews the market. How is more government spending and involvement going to improve that?

Indeed, the Affordable Health Care Act passed in 2010 was touted as a necessary law that would reduce costs. The law passed by Congress was 2000 pages long. The law gave regulation authority to a newly created bureaucracy that wrote thousands of additional pages of regulations. This myriad of new requirements caused medical providers, insurance companies, and businesses to increase their administrative costs to learn about, interpret, implement, and keep records for hundreds of new requirements. This new administrative cost, plus the new government bureaucracy, added to costs of medical care in this country rather than reduced costs.

To think thousands of pages of new laws and regulations piled upon one sector of the economy would somehow reduce costs in that sector is out of touch with the reality of what it takes to operate a business. The rhetoric put forth promoting passage of the Affordable Health Care Act promised the impossible. The greatest danger and challenge our nation faces today is that too many in the electorate believe and accept the rhetoric, and do not hold their representatives accountable for the outcomes of their actions.

I often read or hear things people point to as examples of how the marketplace went bad, or examples of how the government fixed things when markets went bad, but when I look into them, I find that it was just the opposite. What they are stating is not fact, but political rhetoric from one side or the other. That rhetoric becomes popular at the time of the events and survives to eventually become presented as truth. Interpretations of what happened during the Great Depression are classic examples.

Rhetoric today paints President Hoover as a laissez-faire economist, but even prior to his election as president he started to develop a penchant for meddling with business when he served as U.S. Secretary of Commerce. As president, in response to the economic downturn, Hoover increased spending significantly and raised tariffs to such an extent that international trade came to a near standstill. As a result, farmers lost nearly a third of their markets at a time when agriculture represented a significant share of the economy.[32]

Tens of thousands of farms went bankrupt, causing the failure of a vast number of rural banks. During his last year in office, Hoover doubled the average income tax rate, raised other taxes, and created new taxes. He also created the Reconstruction Finance Corporation, which not only subsidized companies but also put in place regulations that controlled how owners conducted their business.

During the presidential campaign of 1932, Roosevelt criticized Hoover for the actions he was taking. Roosevelt's VP running mate, John Nance Garner, warned that Hoover was leading the country down the path to socialism.[33]

Once in office, the Roosevelt administration embarked on a doubling down on the programs that Hoover had started. One of the individuals in Roosevelt's administration responsible for the policies, Rexford Guy Tugwell, stated years later, "We didn't admit it at the time, but practically the whole New Deal was extrapolated from the programs that Hoover started."[34] Although today the Rhetoric seeks to portray the two presidents as significantly different, the facts show them pursuing identical policies.

More recently, we had a government artificially stimulating the economy with risky government-promoted loans. In turn, those loans were securitized. This commingling of borrowed money with securities, something that had been regulated during the 1930s, was deregulated in recent years. At the same time, we had government deficit spending, prompted mostly by a knee-jerk reaction to 9/11 by a Congress and president who needed to appear as if they were doing something. When the markets, led by a housing glut in 2008, finally crashed, it is ironic that many politicians were quick to point to private banks, financial institutions, and other corporations as the culprits, while ignoring their own complicity. They create a rhetoric that distorts or conceals the truth of the matter. By covering up the facts of how we get into a mess, it becomes nearly impossible for many citizens to understand how to get out of it and avoid the same situations in the future.

POLITICAL RHETORIC

Why would politicians want to do this, distort the truth, and mislead the nation with respect to the best path to recovery? Because the rhetoric is developed for political purposes to place the opposing party or others in a bad light, and their own in a positive light, rather than honestly understand what is best for the nation. Rhetoric is developed to win elections.

Unfortunately, most journalists are educated in writing, speaking, and promoting opinions, not in understanding how business and the economy functions. Thus, they report not on the things that bring understanding and solutions, but on what they hear and read from the politicians, the rhetoric, and the political debates.

We get much more reporting today on political strategies and speech than we do on the facts. Reporting on controversial issues such as health care, stimulus spending, and "climate change," discuss the politics behind the discussions, and not the facts of the issue, or the wording of laws being considered. You can listen to news reports on TV for a month and not know what some law being proposed actually states, or will result in, nor will you know much about the technology, science, facts, or history of the issue. You will, however, know all about the political rhetoric.

RHETORIC VS PROSPERITY

In the 1940s, young Americans went abroad to fight a world war and discovered that American self-reliance, ingenuity, and industrial production could win that war. They learned what the nation appeared to forget, that they could accomplish great things and overcome great struggles through their own efforts, and Providence. Many experienced times when they had to rely on themselves, their buddies next to them, and faith in God for their very survival. Their success relied not on some fat cat sitting at a desk in Washington, DC. They also saw the horrible results of absolute government power. They came home with a can-do attitude that had been lost a decade earlier. They went to work, started businesses, and began to rebuild the greatest nation in the world. They celebrated their freedom. They forgot about the rhetoric.

Without realizing it, they had learned the fundamental lesson about the secret of America's greatness: individual freedom, the right to freely engage in private enterprise, and enjoy the benefits from that effort . . . I pray to God we do not have to fight another war to learn this lesson again.

CHAPTER 8

WEALTH AND JOB CREATION

"The preservation of the sacred fire of liberty and the destiny of the republican model of government are justly considered as deeply, perhaps as finally, staked on the experiment entrusted to the hands of the American people."

George Washington, First Inaugural Address, April 30, 1789

THE PRODUCTIVITY KEY

It is unfortunate that so many people, particularly individuals who reach levels of high authority, clearly misunderstand the fundamentals of economies that result in the growth of wealth, and the creation of new jobs and opportunities. It was disappointing to me that President Obama, upon winning the election of 2008, set up an economic advisory committee and openly solicited suggestions about what to do about the economy. More disconcerting was that many thought this was okay.

We should have never gotten into that economic mess, but there should also not have been any great mystery about what to do, especially from someone who had just won an election, promising he had a plan. To know what to do, we need to have some basic understanding.

New permanent jobs are created by a true expansion in the economy—a net increase in the total of goods and services produced by that nation. The total of goods and services our nation produces represents the total wealth of our nation. An increase in the total value of goods and services of an economy, only by inflation, is not an expansion of the economy; the total of goods and services produced are not increased. Thus, an increase in the GDP may or may not reflect an actual increase in the wealth of the nation.

Increasing GDP by government printing or borrowing money, and then spending it on things that do not increase the productive capacity of the nation, such as more bureaucracy, payments to people to not work, or constructing things that are nonproductive, does not create new long-term employment. Printing more money without real wealth creation causes inflation which hurts the average citizen by reducing the value of their money. Beneficiaries include debtors with low fixed interest rates.

The largest debtor in the world is the United States government. Borrowing money by the US government takes capital reserves away from businesses that have the capacity to generate new wealth and redistributes it by arbitrary methods to those favored by politicians who decide who receives and who doesn't.

To increase permanent jobs, the total productive output, our wealth collectively as a nation, needs to increase. Money should be borrowed only for endeavors that will increase productive output. This is done primarily by businesses investing in new plants and equipment.

When considering improving the economy, one should look at what it takes to increase productive output. Adding money artificially does nothing directly to increase total productive output. Looking at the stimulus of the economy from a consumer perspective is completely misguided. The government borrowing dollars or printing dollars is not creating wealth—it is diffusing wealth. Indeed, government borrowing introduces an inefficiency in wealth transfer by adding more middlemen and causing the government to pay interest that becomes a future drag on the economy.

Understanding productivity is key to the solution of new job creation. The total productive capacity of a nation determines the net wealth of the nation. Things that increase productive capacity result in increases in material living standards and reduce unemployment. Productive capacity has limits. The labor productive capacity of a nation is the sum of the productive capacity of all individuals. This total is influenced by many factors, including education levels, attitudes, level of positive socialization, and cooperative spirit.

New technologies often result in increased productivity. Advances in equipment technology have often been mistakenly viewed as causes of job loss. From the perspective of the individual who is no longer needed to do what a robot now does, this is an understandable conclusion. However, from a national perspective, this is incorrect. The increase in productivity of that manufacturing process has now freed up the productive capacity of that individual to produce something else.

The net result, after that person discovers what other useful thing he or she can do, society as a whole gets the benefit of the new good or service he or she is now providing, as well as the old thing now being produced by a robot. This represents an overall increase in our productivity and standard of living.

UNEXPECTED LESSON

Those who view free-market economies with disdain and favor strong centralized federal economic control, a la socialist and Marxist philosophies, should stop to consider the lesson we have confronting us from an unexpected source, China. In the last forty years, China's GDP4 grew over 9000 percent, a rate greater than the United States achieved in the first one hundred years of our nation, during which we surpassed China as the largest economy in the world. To learn the reason for China's extraordinary economic success, the IMF sponsored a study in the 1990s asking the question "Why Is China Growing So Fast?"[35]

After 1978, Chinese authorities made the decision to reform their economic policies. Considerable input into new machinery, better technology, and infrastructure improvements explained a portion of the increase, but it could not account for the majority of the increase that set China apart from the rest of the world's growth rates. Increases in productivity were found to be the key to their phenomenal growth. Increases in productivity occurred as a result of providing the opportunity to individuals and groups to form private businesses allowed to retain profits from their enterprises. The economic expansion was further accelerated by opening the country to foreign investment.

The following quote from the study's conclusion sums up the takeaway lesson for other nations, including the United States,

"Most important, while capital investment is crucial to growth, it becomes even more potent when accompanied by market-oriented reforms that introduce profit incentives to rural enterprises and small businesses. That combination can unleash a productivity boom that will propel aggregate growth."

We overtook China as the world's economic leader in the world 130 years ago. Ninety years later, they learned from us what we forgot and have now retaken the position of the world's largest economy. In the United States, if we desire to continue the prosperity handed to us by our forefathers, we need to learn this lesson of increasing productivity through encouraging and supporting free enterprise as the key to growing the wealth of our nation.

NONPRODUCTIVITY

Not all roles in society result in a positive net productivity. There is a level of nonproductive activity (government and business administration, for example) that is necessary for a stable functioning society, but there is a tendency, particularly in larger organizations and governments, to add more nonproductive roles. This reduces the overall productive capacity of the society.

Some government jobs are essential for the safety and security of the nation, as well as provision of orderly conduct of commerce and transportation. But the US federal government has gone far beyond those necessary functions. There are two primary reasons for this. The first results from politicians unable to say "No" to their constituents who create a new benefit, program, or office of government to make it appear that they are doing something regarding a perceived concern. In some cases, the concern may not even be a reality.

The Department of Education is a classic example of this. The federal government is not charged, and is not responsible, for providing education to the citizenry. Funding and staffing such an agency, and then distributing funds to states through this agency, merely adds another layer of bureaucracy that produces no productive benefit. If states or local school boards determine they need additional funding for their education programs, they have their own funding mechanisms to do so.

The second reason creates benefits for select groups such as unions, corporations, businesses, senior citizens, women, minorities, and professions, to name a few. Each of these represent a special interest group. It appears that both major political parties engage in this patronizing and mercantilist behavior. Most career politicians can be heard criticizing the pandering to special interest groups, but a majority also practice such pandering. Nearly all legislation involves some degree of special interest involvement.

Retirement is another way that societies convert a productive person to a nonproductive liability. It is ironic that one of the original arguments in favor of Social Security was that persons who retired on Social Security would make room in the workforce for others to get that job. This perverted line of thinking ignores the fact that the retired person is no longer a productive contributing tax-paying person, but is now a liability that must be paid for with tax dollars. Every time someone retires on Social Security or a government pension, our national productivity level is reduced, and our societal, economic burden is increased.

SERVICE SECTOR

In the recent past, the United States has seen a significant increase in service sector jobs. Many, including myself, in previous decades, were concerned about the rise of the proportion of service versus manufacturing jobs in our country. However, increases in the service sector were accompanied by increases in manufacturing productivity. Fewer people were needed to produce the same quantity of goods. This increase in productivity enables the nation to expand the total of goods and services, because some individuals have been freed up from the manufacturing process to do other work.

Services can be looked upon in three ways. Services can help increase the productivity of those being served, they can be looked upon as an increase in the standard of living of those being served, or they can be looked upon negatively as a nonproductive use of labor, to provide frivolous luxuries to individuals who could do for themselves and save the expense. How the service should be viewed is determined by how the recipient uses it. I believe, in the last few decades in our nation, we witnessed an overall increase in living standards as our productivity increased due to technological advances. This technological advance enabled an increase in service sector jobs which adds to our living standards.

GOVERNMENT'S ROLE

The problem with the government purposely trying to cause the increase of production to create jobs is that government does not know which goods really need to be produced. Putting money back into the economy by the government can only properly be done by reversing the process by which it collects that money. Taxes should be either lowered or rebated. This presumes that the government has wisely managed the money it receives, and a tax surplus is available to be rebated.

Spending by the government merely for the sake of trying to spend money is always wasteful and nonproductive and should be avoided. Government spending should only be done for items perceived to be proper, prudent, and necessary, after appropriate consideration.

So, what is the government's role in the economy? 1) Provide a stable and secure environment in which to function (defense and law enforcement), and 2) Regulate economic and financial transactions (commerce).

A society needs to be secure in its position as a nation within the world, not under imminent threat of violence from other nations. It needs to have a law-abiding citizenry where businesses can operate without fear of loss of property, goods, or money due to theft, vandals, or riot. Owners must have security in their ownership of property and goods without the threat of confiscation by government.

Equally important is the need for governmental policies and regulations to be stable and consistent. Introducing sweeping new changes in policy, regulation, and additional taxes, imposes an uncertainty upon businesses and individuals that inhibits decisions toward expansion, growth, and new business development.

To promote commerce, the government provides regulations that help maintain the stability and efficiency of transactions within markets without restricting the functioning of supply and demand. Regulation does not mean monetary distribution to individuals or entities from the treasury without in-kind benefit received from the recipients. It does not mean telling businesses what prices they should charge. It does not mean collecting money from citizens on a national level, and then redistributing that money to states for use in what would normally be state functions. Furthermore, it does not mean telling individual citizens how they should provide for their medical care, what they should eat, etc.

National officeholders should remember that the leader of a group accomplishes nothing on his own. A great society is created when leaders seek to empower individuals to maximize their productive and creative outputs, and not self-promotion and claiming personal credit for the accomplishment of others. Individual output is maximized when obstacles such as taxes and regulations are minimized, while incentives are maximized. The greatest incentive is the freedom to pursue your dreams and the financial, mental, emotional, physical, and spiritual benefits that result from such pursuits.

In the preceding paragraphs, I have been referring to government as a faceless entity. This is a trap most of us fall into, and many never recognize. Government is the collection of individuals elected or hired to perform common societal functions as laid out in our Constitution, laws, and regulations. Decisions of government are not made by an all-powerful faceless entity we call government; they are made by people like ourselves. If we place into the hands of government an enterprise, such as financing home loans, or educating children, or providing health care, there are real people making decisions, not some all-knowing government.

For private enterprise owners and employees, their very livelihoods depend upon the decisions they make. Their business decisions determine whether there will be a next paycheck.

Government officials rarely, if ever, are held responsible for the economic impact of their decisions. Their performance is not based upon economic productivity, but rather political or bureaucratic criteria blind to, or in opposition to, increasing productivity. Thus, consigning portions of economic activity to government control removes the incentive from those who make decisions of the need to be productively efficient. Unless a business grows so large that it precludes competition or individual freedom, if job creation and real economic growth are the desire, then direct government control of economic enterprises should be avoided.

CHAPTER 9

POVERTY AND INCOME DISTRIBUTION

"To take from one because it is thought that his own industry and that of his fathers has acquired too much, in order to spare to others, who, or whose fathers have not exercised equal industry and skill, is to violate arbitrarily the first principle of association—the guarantee to every one of a free exercise of his industry and the fruits acquired by it."

Thomas Jefferson, 1816

"For you yourselves know how you ought to imitate us; we were not idle when we were with you, and we did not eat anyone's bread without paying for it; but with toil and labor we worked night and day, so that we might not burden any of you . . . For even when we were with you, we gave you this command: Anyone unwilling to work should not eat. For we hear that some of you are living in idleness, mere busybodies, not doing any work. Now such persons we command and exhort in the Lord Jesus Christ to do their work quietly and to earn their own living. Brothers and sisters do not be weary in doing what is right."

2 Thessalonians 3:7–8,10–13, NRSV

THE ENDLESS WAR

The "War on Poverty" was initiated in 1964 by Congress and President Lyndon Johnson. Those who support the programs to this day claim there are proportionally fewer in poverty than when the programs started. This is only true if you include the value of the government assistance individuals received as part of their income. This argument avoids the truth that such welfare assistance enables many individuals to subsist in their low-income status, marginally above the poverty level, without giving incentive or motivation to become financially self-sufficient.

I'm not opposed to welfare assistance. There are many working individuals whose incomes are marginal, who receive assistance for food and/or health care, who are striving to lift themselves out of their circumstances. I know some mothers with children whose circumstances changed, causing them to require temporary financial assistance.

One case involved a wife and mother of two elementary-aged children whose husband died suddenly. As a full-time mom, she had never worked outside the home. The husband earned a good salary, but they had no significant savings. The man had a life insurance policy, but the settlement of the claim was held up for months by insurance company red tape. The woman lost her house, moved into government-operated low-income housing, and began receiving government financial assistance. Once she received the insurance settlement, she was able to reacquire the house, get training, and begin supporting her family.

The basic social safety net we developed has a place in our society. Unfortunately, many individuals I have encountered that receive assistance abuse the system.

One woman lived in a small rental house. Her working boyfriend lived with her, except on days when a social worker was likely to visit.

She had a daughter of middle school age, qualifying her to receive additional benefits. She mentioned to me a discussion she and her boyfriend had one day, determining that what she made could pay the basic bills, which left his income to party on. Unfortunately, the daughter was exposed to drugs, excessive alcohol, and promiscuity.

After the birth of our youngest son, while my wife was recovering in the hospital, she shared her room with a young woman in her 20s. The nurse filling out the form with birth certificate information came in and asked what the child's name would be. The young mother had a name but did not know how to spell it. She said they would have to contact the father. They weren't married and did not live together. He was found across town in a bar, getting drunk.

Her mother then visited, leading a gaggle of little toddlers, all belonging to the young mother. The discussion with her mother centered around the increase in assistance they'd receive, now that she had her fifth child.

Finally, the doctor came in and talked to her about going on birth control, but she wasn't interested. My wife was aghast by what she saw and heard.

After the young woman left to go home, my wife asked the doctor how often he sees this. "All the time," he replied. He estimated forty percent of his deliveries involved young unwed mothers on assistance. For a year after that, I watched the newspaper and noted all the new birth announcements. The number of young single mothers was almost exactly forty percent.

The last two stories are from the early 1990s. There have been reforms and changes to our welfare system through the years, but fundamentally the assistance levels have continued. In more recent years, I worked as a volunteer, serving meals to homeless and low-income individuals and families. I conclude through the people I met that there will always be a need for assistance for some, but also that abuses of the system continue today.

The tragedy is that children are raised in this system. The examples they experience of how to earn a living have to do with receiving government assistance. Our War on Poverty has been going on for more than fifty years. The children of that young woman in the hospital are now raising children of their own. Some raising them up in the only way they know, by government assistance. After fifty years, we are now supporting the third or fourth welfare generation in this country.

SOURCES OF POVERTY

Poverty on a national scale is caused by a lack of freedom and/or poor governance. In the absence of these two causes, poverty is caused mostly by poor socialization of the individual, either at home, in schools, or both. The result breeds ignorance of what it takes to stay gainfully employed and how to handle money. It can also result in a poor attitude that results in a lack of motivation, or worse, a belief that they're a victim of circumstances that they cannot rise above.

People in the US aren't forced to live that way. In many poverty cases, it's a result of how they're raised and the choices they make in their life. People are a combination of their genetic makeup, upbringing, and the environment in which they live. That includes the people they choose to associate with.

Poverty on a personal scale, with the exception of a small minority of handicapped and disabled individuals, is a matter of attitude and perceptions. I know individuals who have no understanding of how to manage money. They have no appreciation of planning and tracking spending, budgeting, and saving money. They spend what income they have, make no plans for future expenditures or unplanned life events, and then bemoan that they have no money. They wallow in their poverty, when in fact, it's self-inflicted.

I know others who, in some cases, have less income than the people I describe above, who have an abundance of material things and money. The difference is how they manage the money they do have. Many are poor because they have no understanding of how to manage money. They believe rich people are rich because of their income. To the contrary, most people who have significant net monetary worth results from the money that they retained, not necessarily by how much they earned.

This lack of understanding explains why there are so many cases of individuals who win the lottery, but then go on to become bankrupt. We also see prominent individuals who make millions in the sports or entertainment industries, yet end up filing bankruptcy.

The solution to this problem is *education*: *education* of all citizens regarding how the economy really works; *education* of how enterprises are conceived, created, operated, and expanded; *education* on the importance of the freedoms we possess to pursue our dreams in private enterprise.

PURSUING THE AMERICAN DREAM

If you want to end poverty, stop enabling people to remain in their poverty by funding that lifestyle. Also stop lowering educational standards and expectations for the average student. Instead, teach them how to escape their situation. Teach them discipline and a positive attitude. Teach them proper management of money and positive work ethics. Teach them the importance of learning; the reasons for fundamental skills in language, mathematics, science, and technology, so that they can be of greater value to employers, have the skills to develop their own business, and possess and acquire the knowledge needed to be responsible citizens. Teach them about the freedoms that they have, how a free society with free markets work, and how they can pursue their dreams within our free society.

But do not mislead them. Make sure they know hard work and vigilance is needed, because freedom includes the freedom to fail. The knowledge of the possibilities of failure provides strong incentive to work diligently to avoid such failure, and go on to be successful. Teach them of past successes by others, including those who failed in first attempts, but persevered to eventually succeed in realizing their dreams. Finally, don't neglect to teach morality in the conduct of business and economic affairs. Honesty and integrity!

It is time we stop denigrating our nation and stop focusing only on whatever faults or flaws we may find. It is time we return to recognizing the special place our nation has in the history of mankind; this special nation which our predecessors thankfully credited as a gift from God himself.

We have been given this rare and precious gift by our founders and ancestors, who sacrificed so much, even their very lives, to create and preserve the freedoms we have. They include the freedom to associate and the freedom to speak, and the freedom to build a dream, and benefit financially from the fruits of that dream. This freedom had a name when I was growing up. It was called the American Dream. It is time that we restore that dream to our nation and our children.

CHAPTER 10

GOVERNMENT TAXES, SPENDING, AND DEBT

"As a very important source of strength and security, cherish public credit. One method of preserving it is, to use it as sparingly as possible; avoiding occasions of expense by cultivating peace, but remembering also that timely disbursements to prepare for danger frequently prevent much greater disbursements to repel it; avoiding likewise the accumulation of debt, not only by shunning occasions of expense, but by vigorous exertions in time of peace to discharge the debts, which unavoidable wars may have occasioned, not ungenerously throwing upon posterity the burden, which we ourselves ought to bear."

George Washington, Farewell Address, September 17, 1796

"The consequences arising from the continual accumulation of public debts in other countries ought to admonish us to be careful to prevent their growth in our own."

John Adams, First Address to Congress, November 23, 1797

"It is incumbent on every generation to pay its own debts as it goes."

Thomas Jefferson, December 26, 1820

A BRIEF HISTORY

I believe the average American today is not aware of the true magnitude of the debt we have accumulated, or of the staggering rate it continues to grow, unless Congress and the president work together to address the issue. The last time the national debt of the United States federal government went down in real terms was in 1957. In the latter part of the 1990s, the growth of the debt was stopped temporarily by a Congress controlled by Republicans. Then came the attack on the World Trade Center and the Pentagon in 2001, and the Republican-controlled Congress and President Bush created a new department and increased spending in the name of "Homeland Security."

In 2007, Democrats retook control of Congress. President Obama entered office in 2009, during the advent of a recession that the news media promoted as the worst recession since the Great Depression. A *Time* magazine cover depicted Obama's head imposed upon a picture of Franklin Roosevelt, with an article suggesting what Obama could learn from Roosevelt; reinforcing the narrative of the Great Recession that President Obama faced. Unfortunately, with both houses of Congress and the office of the president under the control of one party, the Democrats took items from Roosevelt's playbook, and spending by the federal government soared. Much of this was unnecessary.

I provide a couple of charts here to illustrate the magnitude of the rate of growth of the debt.[36] On these graphs, I include off-budget intergovernmental as well as public obligations of the federal government. The off-budget items are mostly money invested by the Social Security system in federal bonds.

Some disregard the Social Security obligations because they represent loans to ourselves. This is a deceptive premise. Those obligations represent cash collected by the federal government and then expended.

That accumulation of capital is gone. American taxpayers sometime in the future are going to have to pay that debt with interest.

Others see the collection of funds and distributing them into the economy as stimulation of the economy. Over the long term, this churning of dollars creates a drag on the economy, rather than a stimulus. It appears to stimulate, but the reality is a portion of the funds go to pay for the bureaucracy to administrate the system, and the system removes capital that could otherwise fund actual wealth-generating investments. To keep this system going, more money is printed that makes the GDP appear to increase, but in reality inflation is caused by excessive government spending.

The first chart in Figure 1 shows the total federal debt, including off-budget items per person in the United States, in unadjusted dollars. I am using dollars unadjusted for inflation because, in the next figure, we are going to look at ratios of items by year, and compare the change in ratios over time. In 1967, the debt per person was $1,640.70. In the previous ten years, the debt level had been relatively steady in unadjusted terms, but in 1967 it started to climb, and never looked back. Note that this corresponds, among other things, to the ramping up of the Vietnam War, and the implementation of the War on Poverty.

In 2019, the debt per person was $69,185.90 and climbing fast. There are three interesting sections of the curve to note. First, in the later 1990s, the curve flattened out, indicating the debt ceased rising. If we used real dollars, it would show a slight decline heading toward the year 2000.

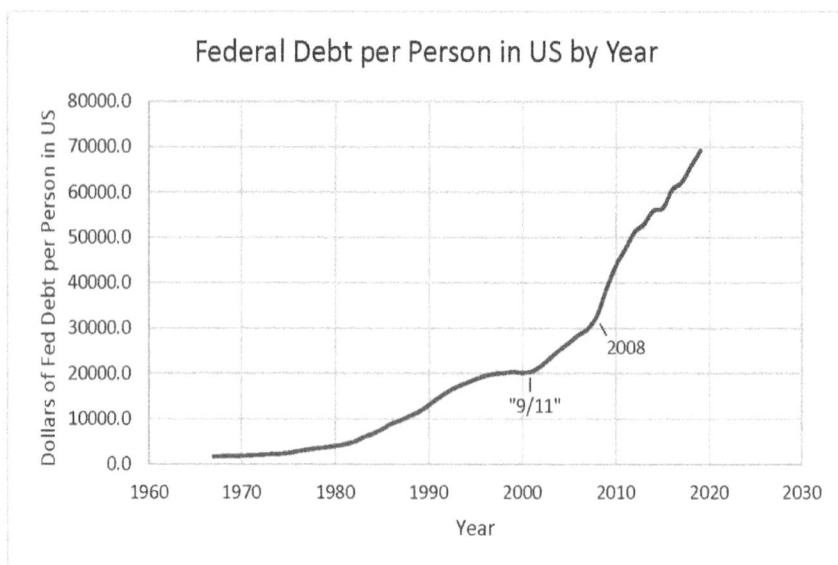

Figure 1. United States Federal Debt Per
Person by Year, 1967 to 2019.

    This time period occurs during the Clinton administration, with a Republican Congress, many of whom entered office with an advertised mandate called the Contract with America. The first item in the Contract was a balanced budget amendment. The amendment did not pass, but the Republican-held Congress successfully curtailed spending to bring the budget under control. After having efforts to increase spending rebuffed by Congress, the Clinton administration joined in the effort with what they referred to as Reinventing Government.

    The progress on the debt abruptly ended on September 11, 2001, less than a year into the George W. Bush presidency. Following the 9/11 attacks on the World Trade Center and the Pentagon, the president and Congress responded swiftly. Spending grew significantly, resulting in a steady increase in the federal debt throughout the Bush presidency.

    In 2007, Democrats regained control of Congress. In 2008, the subprime mortgage crisis hit the country and Barack Obama was elected president. The reaction to recession fueled by the housing market glut, and accompanying magnification of mortgage defaults, was to open the federal government checkbook even wider. This led to a dramatic increase in the federal debt.

The second chart in Figure 2 compares the percent of increase in debt over time to percentage increases in average home price, median income, and GDP. Proportionally, the federal debt rises dramatically relative to the other parameters. Since 1967, the federal debt has increased nearly 7,000 percent. It rose roughly three-and-a-half times more than home costs and the GDP, and nearly seven times more than the median income. More troubling, the trend of these lines does not seem to be changing. The trends displayed in Figure 2 are untenable. Our economic day of reckoning is coming. The longer we leave these trends unabated, the future financial impact on Americans worsens.

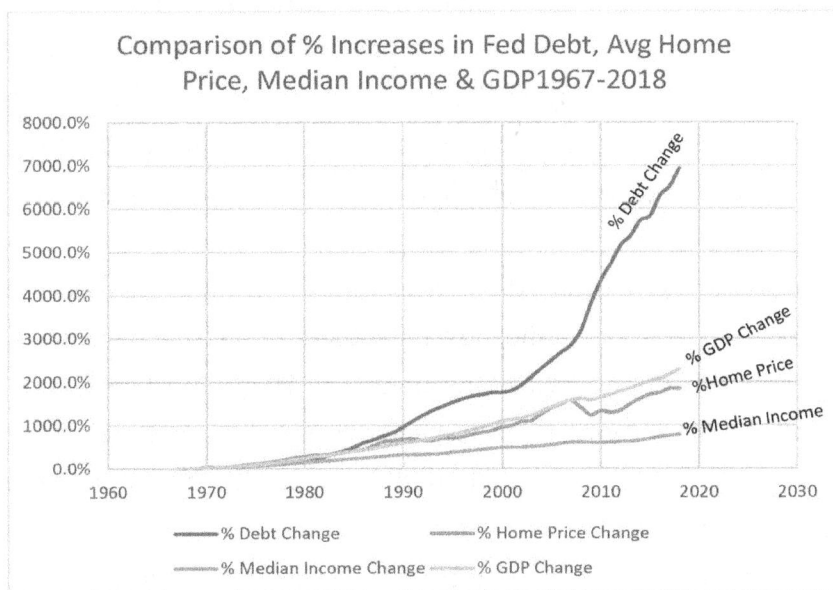

Comparison of % Increases in Fed Debt, Avg Home Price, Median Income & GDP1967-2018

Figure 2. Percent Increase in Federal Debt, Average Home Price, GDP and Median Income, By Year 1967–2018.

WHY WORRY?

Franklin Roosevelt waved away critics of increasing the national debt by saying that it was all owed to Americans, so that we'd be paying it back to Americans with interest. This fallacious thinking assumes the debt is paid back within a beneficial time frame in real dollars, with the same or greater buying power as when borrowed. Further, as pointed out earlier, that money borrowed by the government reduces funds available to investments for increasing wealth-generating productive output.

The federal government, during most of the modern times, managed debt by increasing the money supply. This does not reduce debt. It just makes it look smaller compared to the rising cost of everything else. Furthermore, in today's world, nearly thirty percent of the US debt is owned by foreign investors and governments. The largest foreign owner of US debt in 2020 is China, hardly a nation concerned about our national interests. The argument that we are just borrowing from ourselves is no longer valid. Indeed, the time frame for repaying, or even just inflating the debt away, is so long that we borrow not from just ourselves, but from our children, our grandchildren, and our great grandchildren.

Many do not concern themselves with the national debt because it doesn't appear to significantly affect them in their personal lives. The economy still seems to bump along. The danger and damage debt inflicts does not come all at once, and the detrimental effects are not perceptible directly. Debt is an invisible enemy that slowly sucks the life out of our economy.

When borrowing money in any sort of significant quantity, whether buying a home, or financing a national debt, you draw from a pool of money representing significant time, effort, and resources to accumulate. On a national scale, this pile of money represents millions of individual's effort and savings.

The quantity of money in the current national debt of the United States represents a rare and precious thing, extremely difficult to acquire. When the federal government takes such a large block of money and spends it, that rare and precious thing is gone, forever. It will take another significant effort on the part of millions of individuals to reacquire that quantity of cash into one place again. Meanwhile, that quantity which the government takes and diffuses is not available for anyone else to use.

The "anyone else" includes all the private industries and businesses that might have plans to construct new facilities, expand businesses, buy new equipment, for which they could then hire new employees to operate and be productive. But now they find it difficult to borrow that money, because the piles of cash available to borrow have been diminished. The basis upon which businesses make their decisions on where to spend the money are based upon consumer demand, and thus have a much greater chance to produce things that are needed and desired, leading to a successful productive enterprise. Government-driven spending is based upon political motivations separated from the reality of the marketplace, and thus have a much greater propensity to fail to increase the nation's wealth.

There are only three options for the government to sustain deficit spending. The first is to do nothing to relieve the money supply crunch, which will absolutely kill the economy, and is what happened in the early 1930s. The second is to borrow money which may provide a short-term stimulus but soon thereafter hampers recovery and inhibits long-term economic growth.

Third is to create more money. When this is done, since the net productive capacity of the nation has not changed, the net value of each dollar becomes less. As stated before, this is inflation.

Most think of a little inflation as a healthy indicator for the economy and unavoidable in a growing economy. I completely disagree. In a rapidly advancing technological economy such as ours, the trend should be deflationary. The vast strides in technology in the last several decades should greatly increase our individual productivity. Increases in productivity lower unit costs of production and, in turn, enable lower prices.

The only significant reason for inflation in the last few decades is government borrowing money for expenses, well beyond the means of the government to pay, and this ultimately lowers the unit value of the currency. Wages and other costs rise out of necessity to keep up with the lowering value of the dollar. It is an extreme tragedy that the greatest nation in the history of the earth has squandered this great technological advancement in productivity to the point where we find ourselves.

WINNERS AND LOSERS

It is important to note that with each scenario of inflation and deflation, there are winners and losers. Deflation is good for consumers of new products. Deflation driven by increased productivity lowers the cost of living and thus increases our standard of living. Deflation is not good for long-term debts and certain investments.

The converse is true for inflation. With inflation, a debt incurred becomes easier to pay off with inflated dollars, and long-term investments, such as your house, gain in value. However, inflation causes costs for necessities to rise, lowering the overall standard of living. Individuals on fixed incomes suffer most from inflation. Inflation favors those with large debts and those with significant amounts of investments in things that appreciate with inflation. A government with significant debt will favor policies in the direction of inflation. In the private sector, it is wealthy individuals who benefit most from excessive government spending and out-of-control government debt.

Ironically, "liberal" policies that claim to help poorer citizens put more pressure to incur large government debt. That debt creates inflation that lowers living standards that, in proportion, negatively impacts the poorest citizens the most. There are many that decry the widening gap between rich and poor in our nation, and that to rectify this situation the "wealthy" should be taxed more. This will not solve the widening gap. If the gap is indeed widening, the solution should be to address the cause of runaway government spending.

Some may argue that we haven't really seen significant inflation and so what I am saying is not correct. That logic ignores the vast technological increases that work to lower consumer costs. The cost of producing certain goods has gone down significantly due to technological advances, but we do not see that, because the value of the dollar has been decreasing due to increased government spending. Without the great productivity revolution we've experienced in the last few decades, we'd be experiencing inflation manifested in out-of-control rising consumer prices. To see how inflation manifests itself, consider the typical young American family's ability to buy a new home thirty-five years ago versus today.

In 1985, the median income was $23,618, the average home price per square foot was about $51.84, and the federal debt per person in the US was $7,663. Estimates for the year 2020 are median income of $65,000, average home price of $156.67 per square foot, and the federal debt per person about $72,600. The average inflation rate from 1985 to 2020 gives one dollar in 1985 equal to $2.40 in 2020. The median income during that period increased 275 percent, theoretically staying ahead of inflation, but the average home price per square foot increased just over 300 percent in thirty years. The typical new home today is also larger than in the past, thus magnifying a young couple's difficulty in buying a home.

The cost of new home construction rising faster than inflation and median income is explained in the fact that home construction has not benefited as greatly from the increase in technology as other sectors of the economy. Robotics have not replaced the need for carpenters, concrete workers, block masons, roofers, etc. Further, production of some of the basic raw materials used in home construction are still produced using comparable technology to thirty-five years ago. Thus, despite the great gains in technology-driven productivity in the last thirty-five years, median- and lower-income individuals are getting squeezed out of the home buying market.

What is causing that squeeze? Look at the increase in federal debt from 1985 to 2020. The increase per person from $7,663 to $72,600 is an increase of about 950 percent. That is nearly four times the rate of inflation! You cannot do this without causing the dollar to lose real value. That loss is going to manifest itself somewhere. The cost of homes is one place where it can be seen.

The squeezing of new home buyers creates greater pressure on borrowing in the private sector. Home buyers must commit a greater percentage of their income, and finance a larger mortgage relative to their annual salary than in the past, to buy a typical home. This is due both to inflation driving costs for homes up faster than increasing wages, and to the typical home being built larger than in the past. This two-fold increase exacerbates our precarious debt position as a nation. Increasing debt at all levels undermines the ability to grow and advance the productivity and wealth of our nation.

MORTGAGING OUR NATION

Another significant aspect of our economy that keeps inflation seemingly low is the relocation of manufacturing of goods to foreign countries, particularly China. In many cases the wages paid and working conditions provided to produce the goods we buy in the United States would be totally unacceptable if those wages and conditions were employed here in our country. We all as a nation have been content to turn a blind eye to this inequity, and continue to consume those goods produced under conditions we would not approve of for ourselves. I believe this is a moral as well as an economic issue we need to recognize.

I am not in favor of imposing tariffs as protectionist measures to shelter inefficient domestic producers. I am a believer in free trade, but it should be *fair* free trade. Over half of the trade deficit in 2019 was from China. The second-highest deficit was with Mexico. The two combined accounted for nearly three-fourths of the total US trade deficit. Wages and working conditions in both these countries are poor compared to the US. Tariffs and the threat of tariffs should be tied to creating a more even playing field, improving employee pay and work environments in those nations. If all the goods we purchase from these countries were produced using the costs we experience here in the US, we would realize the full impact of the inflationary effects of the debt we're creating.

The trade deficits are funded by private and public debt. The ability to incur debt without constraints insulated us from the effects of our irresponsible behavior. Just like an addictive drug, continuing and deepening reliance on debt becomes an addiction cycle, extremely difficult to break. As a society, we are addicted to debt. And just like drug addiction, this debt addiction has far-reaching damaging impacts. In the last thirty years, the federal debt has grown from just over fifty percent of GDP to over one hundred percent of GDP.

For comparison, last year China's government debt was about fifty-four percent of GDP, and Russia's was just fourteen percent of GDP.[37] Governments with lower debt ratios place themselves in a stronger position to weather significant economic downturns. Now consider where that puts the US, relative to our world power competitors.

In addition to the economic concerns, the transfer of production overseas has become a national security concern. We now depend on foreign sources for many critical materials, medicines, and technical devices. We rely on China for a wide variety of items, including security critical technology products. This is truly foolishness on our part.

The transfer of productive capacity overseas trades our wealth and job-generating capacity at home for corporate profits and lower-cost goods. This shortsighted deal with the devil will eventually catch up with us. I fear that day is coming soon, if it has not already arrived.

This is like the story we read in Genesis 25:29–34 when Esau trades his birthright to Jacob for a bowl of soup, because of his hunger. Esau sought to satisfy his short-term hunger, and failed to consider in the years to come that his birthright would be of significant value to him. This lesson took place nearly 4,000 years ago.

As I write this paragraph on March 20, 2020, the United States is taking radical steps to limit the spread of the coronavirus. The measures being employed include travel restrictions, limits on restaurants and other enterprises, requirements by many states to close selected businesses, and orders for citizens to stay in their homes. These measures impose a tremendous negative impact on the economy. At a time of lost government revenues, Congress and the president approve large federal spending packages. Our already overextended deficit rises even more dramatically. Our failure to exercise restraint in years past and use times of positive economic growth to build up fiscal reserves makes responding to such a crisis as this more difficult and economically disastrous.

The full effect of massive debt on the economy has never been fully appreciated, because the strength of the American economy masks the detrimental effects. We experience limited growth and think we are okay, but the potential wealth generation capacity of the United States is much greater than the marginal growth we experience. That is because we drag a giant anchor of debt that holds us down, compromises our national security, and our children's and grandchildren's futures. To truly make America great again, we must come to grips with our debt and restore our full domestic wealth-generating capacity.

CHAPTER 11

THE AMERICAN PUBLIC SERVANT

"There is danger from all men. The only maxim of a free government ought to be to trust no man living with power to endanger the public liberty."

John Adams, 1772

"Do not put your trust in princes, in mortals, in whom there is no help. When their breath departs, they return to the earth; on that very day their plans perish."

Psalm 146:3–4, NRSV

"Give me now wisdom and knowledge to go out and come in before this people, for who can rule this great people of yours?"

Solomon's Request to God, 2 Chronicles 1:10, NRSV

"We have rights, as individuals, to give as much of our own money as we please to charity; but as members of Congress we have no right so to appropriate a dollar of public money."[38]

David Crockett, US Congressman, died defending the Alamo

AN OPTIMISTIC HOPE

I began writing much of this section just after the November 2, 2010, national election. The conclusions I draw are as valid today as they were then. Ten years later, my optimistic hopes have yet to be fulfilled, but for the sake of my children, grandchildren, and this nation as a harbor of freedom, I must uphold that optimistic hope.

It appeared a sea change occurred politically in the two years leading up to the 2010 election, although I believe perhaps not as much as some might think. In 2008, Mr. Obama ran a campaign based upon change. I knew several people who chose to vote for him with the sole reason they felt it was time for a change. I believe during the following two years, many people realized that things had not really changed, and the perception of some is that things got worse.

The reality is that in 2008 we changed the party of the president, but the control of Congress stayed the same. We elected a president of the same party as that controlling Congress, and thus removed a check and balance as envisioned by the Founding Fathers. In addition, those controlling Congress and the president himself did not seem to promote the goodness of our nation, and what most in the United States would consider our core beliefs. They include the importance of individual freedom, self-reliance, and the sacred trust and responsibility that we hold as the safe harbor of freedoms, human rights, and liberty in a world that is largely ignorant, indifferent, or hostile to such rights and freedoms.

Something seems lost in this nation that once fiercely demanded and defended individual independence. Perhaps the election in 2010 signifies this defining and distinguishing characteristic of Americans, although misplaced, is not completely dead and gone. I choose the optimist's view that before us awaits a new era of growth and celebration of the goodness and greatness of the United States of America.

This optimistic hope will not become a reality without intentional and purposeful action on the part of millions of Americans. It is one thing to have an election where people come together to vote for a change in Congress or the presidency, it is quite another to have a meaningful, positive, and lasting impact on the quality and welfare of our great nation. The actions of representatives to the various elective offices, both nationally and locally, need to be scrutinized and considered when deciding if they should remain in office. The responsibilities of those offices should not for a moment be taken for granted or squandered.

The need for integrity, honor, and righteousness in the conduct of these officeholders has always been great, but now more than ever the need cries out for the utmost efforts on the part of each individual concerned. The need also calls to millions of Americans to selflessly demand of their representatives not privilege, favor, or spoils, but straightforward truth, courageous decision, and moral behavior, because they are the ones that represent us.

This requires on the part of all Americans a radical change in our perceptions and beliefs regarding what constitutes a good representative or elected executive. I recently heard a woman praying sincerely that God would guide us as we vote for those who would rule over us. This prayer deeply concerned me, not because she was seeking guidance for us as voters, but because she sees those whom we are voting for as rulers over us.

Our nation is not governed by rulers. The elected offices are not high stations of privilege and autonomous authority. We're ruled by a Constitution that places limited powers upon a collective body of representatives, intended to hold office in service to their nation and its citizens. They are to be public servants.

The idea that an elected representative is a public servant seems to have become lost in America. Leading up to the 2010 election, the Tea Party movement, and the general disillusionment of many citizens with our political leaders, particularly Congress and the president, was a direct response to the arrogance, patronage, populism, and partisan posturing that has become rampant. The same sentiments of disillusionment and distrust of the entrenched politicians and bureaucrats in Washington, DC helped to sweep Donald Trump into the presidency in 2016.

PATRONAGE, POLITICAL POPULISM AND PARTY POLITICS

The last paragraph identifies three behaviors in professional politicians I find detestable. The first, patronage, can come in many forms. It can be political appointments or favors granted to supporters or friends. It occurs as funding earmarked for a favored project. It appears in legislation passed that provides money or some other legislative benefit to a selected group of people. In the case of the federal government, I have yet to find within the Constitution the justification for the provision of funds to many of the programs it now supports.

Most legislation passed in my lifetime claiming to support the best interests of the American People actually represents work by special interests. Both Democrats and Republicans have been complicit in this. This is not to say that no good can come from a special interest's position, but their position must be taken as one point of view or perspective.

The entire concept of politicians making promises of some new program, or expenditure on a certain project, is patronizing. I have attended several ribbon cuttings and ground breakings on public works projects, and they all follow the same agenda. A variety of politicians stand up and speak to the crowd and cameras, thanking other politicians for their hard work in providing the funding for the project, ignoring the fact that the money they are discussing did not originate from them. I have yet to hear any politician at one of these events thank the people who actually paid for the project—American taxpayers!

The second is political populism. I define political populism as the rhetoric, positions, and actions taken by politicians that represent a course not based in fact, but in emotional sentiment of a certain segment of society. Its intent is in placating and garnering the voting support of that segment of society, with no honest regard for the ultimate outcome of the actions proposed.

Political populism placates one segment of society by vilifying another. We most often see and hear in the nation from politicians, vilifying the rich by promising to make "them" pay. Political populist actions invariably are rife with unintended consequences that do more harm than good to the very people they promise to benefit.

The behavior includes actions and decisions based on the agenda of a political party, not the best benefit of the nation. Political loyalty is meaningless and detrimental if it runs contrary to the best interest of society. Associating with a particular political party is not automatically a bad thing. It becomes damaging when the focus becomes forming policy and legislation merely because it is what the party wants, or worse, what the other party doesn't want.

When a position no longer represents what is in the best interest of the nation, then individual representatives need to have the political courage to stand up and say, "No, this is not right." Using Obamacare as an example, passing a 2,000-+ page law that fundamentally changes how the nation deals with a significant segment of our economy without any meaningful debate, or even having read the bill and understanding what it says and how it impacts us, is reckless and irresponsible. It should be a source of shame for any honest individual that voted for the Affordable Health Care Act in 2010, without demanding at least more time and debate to consider the content and potential consequences of the act before passage.

At the end of 2019, the same party under the same House majority party leadership voted to impeach President Trump, with essentially no public presentation or debate of evidence of criminal wrongdoing that would justify impeachment. I did not vote for Mr. Trump in 2016, but my observations of the Democrat Party in the three-plus years since his election demonstrates to me that their motivation has nothing to do with the best interests of the citizens of this nation. Democrats have sought to impeach him since the day he was elected and have even gone so far as to change the rules of the electoral process to prevent him from running or winning reelection in 2020.

In their party-driven hatred, they set horrific precedents, without regard for the rule of law, open and fair proceedings, honesty, and the truth. In their reckless pursuit of power and control, they fail to see that the over-the-top precedents they set could ultimately be used against them, to their own demise. Their irrational behavior and pursuit of personal and party agendas is out of control. If they ever had any notion of elected office as public service, it is now nowhere to be seen.

MORE CONSIDERATIONS

On the federal level, just because something sounds good, that doesn't make it beneficial for Congress to support it financially. For example, Congress doles out money to local communities for which politicians then claim the credit. The "Scarcity of Resources" in a community forces that community to make tough decisions regarding priorities. Federal programs subvert that process by allowing communities to avoid hard decisions about prioritizing community needs.

Legislators and government executives often overlook or ignore the evaluation of current laws, policies, and practices. The business I work for is always undergoing assessment and reevaluation of how it functions. We make changes in response to such assessments to become more efficient and competitive. This is an ongoing process. Successful businesses do this as a matter of course. Otherwise, they become inefficient, wither, and go out of business.

Government does not follow this process. In government, a new law creates a program with corresponding rules and procedures. As new problems arise, new rules are created. Bureaucrats duly enforce the regulations methodically and systematically. Following procedures and enforcing the rules become ends unto themselves, even if conditions and reason dictate otherwise.

No incentive exists for government workers to change or improve the system, because their job is not threatened by inefficiency. They are judged by how well they follow procedures and enforce the rules, not by how efficiently the system works collectively. This problem becomes most acute when faced with a program that has outlived its intended purpose. The people involved have no incentive to stand up and say, "We are wasting society's money by being here. Lay us off and close down this program."

Evaluating existing government activities should be a routine part of a legislator's responsibilities. This should include assessment of existing programs to determine inefficiencies that require fixing and which ones to eliminate. Unfortunately, many lawmakers do not consider this aspect of their job. Instead, they focus on creating more new laws, adding to the overwhelming regulatory burden that citizens and businesses must bear.

As the volumes of regulations increase, without responsible evaluation of their overall impact, the efficiency of the economy in general diminishes. Ironically, in today's world, many look upon big businesses as bad, yet the great regulatory burden we created greatly favors large businesses that can afford the overhead necessary to cope with the regulations.

In his State of the Union address in 1817, President James Monroe discussed the need to review taxes routinely, as a matter of course, to determine whether they are still needed, and if not, they should be eliminated. His advice appears more valid today than over 200 years ago:

> "It appearing in a satisfactory manner that the revenue arising from imposts and tonnage and from the sale of the public lands will be fully adequate to the support of the civil Government. . . . without the aid of the internal taxes, I consider it my duty to recommend to Congress their repeal. To impose taxes when the public exigencies require them is an obligation of the most sacred character, especially with a free people. The faithful fulfillment of it is among the highest proofs of their value and capacity for self-government. To dispense with taxes when it may be done with perfect safety is equally the duty of their representatives."

QUESTIONS FOR THE PUBLIC SERVANT

Public servants must constantly remind themselves of who they serve. Politicians easily get caught up in the headiness of high authority.

Humility is a behavior that requires cultivation and nurturing, particularly in those who strive for a high position.

Remember who and what you serve:

- The nation's best interest
- The citizens
- The taxpayers
- The Constitution
- The moral higher authority (God)

The above are not in order of importance—they are all important. With these in mind, I offer a few questions for decision-making for elected public servants when considering any legislation:

1. Does this increase freedom?
2. Is it fiscally sound? Does it serve to increase our productive capacity and standard of living?
3. Does it protect the rights and freedoms of *all* individuals?
4. Does it conform to the Constitution? (There is explicit purpose in the restrictions enumerated in the Constitution.)
5. Is it consistent with ensuring the security of our nation? (Driving the nation into bankruptcy is a sure route to destruction of our security.)
6. What are the potential unintended consequences?
7. Are there any unknowns, and if so, are they worth the risk?
8. Is it right? Is it well with your soul?

DO NOT ESTABLISH YOUR GENEROSITY WITH OTHER PEOPLE'S MONEY

It is not uncommon to see one of our politicians standing before a new building or other feature, representing the expenditure of a considerable sum of taxpayers' money and claim personal credit for this "good thing" which he or she has provided for us. Many go further with this self-promotion by promising that they will do this or that if elected or reelected, generally promising to spend more taxpayer's money. The notion of elected officials being public servants seems lost in our country.

Several problems exist with current thinking regarding the role of elected representatives. First, it is not their money. They're not dukes and lords put in place to dole out favors and monetary largess, as they deem appropriate. It's money that millions of hard-working individuals labored countless hours to enable its accumulation into the treasuries of the myriad government coffers housed by our nation.

The spending of any taxpayer money should be taken as a serious event, and never taken lightly or done quickly. Just as the commitment of troops to go serve in harm's way should be done with the utmost deliberation and seriousness, I suggest that nearly the same level of gravity should be applied when considering whether we should spend taxpayer money. If elected officials would adopt this attitude regarding the money they have been entrusted with, an attitude of humble servant rather than arrogant patron, I think they will be more circumspect in their decisions.

Second, it's not their money. There should be no right of legislative bodies to commit future taxpayers to debts and taxes. This is taxation without representation. Ongoing expenses should be paid out of established revenue sources. One-time capital expenditures should be made using the same sources, surplus revenues, or properly placed bond sales. It is inappropriate to approve the expenditure of large sums of money beyond established revenues, and then ask where the money will come from; or worse, leave it up to the Treasury Department, the Federal Reserve, or some made-up committee to come up with the financing. This is the epitome of irresponsibility. At the federal level, both Democrats and Republicans have been complicit in this type of folly from 2002 to present.

Third, it is not their money. Elected officials all over the nation are claiming credit for all manner of goodness, generosity, great things done by them, more legislation, new programs, more buildings and roads, more money given to more people. The problem is . . . it is *not* their money. You do not go into a store or someone else's house and start handing things out to other people from off the shelves as if it is yours to give. Giving gifts to someone that was paid for by others is not generosity. I have been a public representative. It is an important and grave responsibility. One should not take pride in having caused the expenditure of other people's hard-earned money. It should be done with great consideration, care, concern, deliberation, and humility.

CHAPTER 12

DISCONNECTS

"The trouble with the world is not that people know too little; it's that they know so many things that just aren't so."

Mark Twain (Samuel Langhorne Clemens, 1835-1910)

"Fools think their own way is right, but the wise listen to advice."

Proverbs 12:15, The Bible, NRSV

"Reasoning will never make a man correct an ill opinion, which by reasoning he never acquired"

Jonathan Swift, January 9, 1720

MUCH OF PUBLIC DISCOURSE in recent decades suffers from a disconnect between perceptions and reality. In nearly all controversies, one or both sides may be disconnected from reality, but based upon their own perceptions, they both consider themselves justified in their words and actions. There is normally truth or fact in portions of the arguments on both sides, but the disconnected frames of reference cause one or both sides to fail to come to grips with the real problem. The following parable illustrates a disconnect in our discussions regarding education in the United States.

THE EDUCATION BOARD—A PARABLE

It was a Tuesday night. A larger than usual crowd gathered in the audience for the monthly public-school board meeting. Herb Andrews, a junior member of the board, noted this as he took his seat in the front, facing the group. He knew some parents had had enough of the mediocre ratings of their local schools. He heard them on a local radio talk show. They felt the teachers could do a better job. They said the students lacked discipline in the schools, and administrators simply did not do what was necessary to keep classes orderly. The students languished because they lacked the positive environment and motivated educators necessary for quality learning.

The parents rallied a group of concerned citizens who were now here before him and the rest of the board to voice their complaints. After the starting formalities common to most boards and commissions, the public comment time began. Many signed up ahead of time to voice their concerns. Although a time limit of three minutes per person constrained individual comments, the public input period droned on for over an hour.

During that time, the board members were allowed to ask questions of the speakers. There were few questions asked by most members, but Herb asked a few questions of each one who had children in school. He did so in a polite and positive supporting way, but he was actually taking a poll. What he determined from his questioning was that most of these parents had children who were at least average or better in school. The few who had kids "struggling" in school appeared to have an attitude strongly negative toward the system in general, school or otherwise.

This confirmed what he already determined from his own experiences with his children in the school system, as well as from interviews with teachers since he began his term on the board. Children who did well in school had parents who valued their education and encouraged them to do well. Children who did poorly, more often, had parents who were not supportive of their children or the educational system. Children bring the attitudes that were instilled in them from home to the classroom, and their attitude and how much support they received at home were the primary factors for determining their performance.

If all children in the school district had parents as concerned about education as those present in the room that night, then the district would have some of the highest scores in the state, perhaps the nation. What was missing at the meeting were the parents who were unconcerned with their children's performance in school.

Herb was no fool. He could not tell these parents, "Well, the biggest problem we have in our schools is the parents." He would be shouted out of the building. So, he sat with the rest of the board politely taking his veiled poll, nodding his head in active listening mode to the parents voicing their concerns.

This discussion brought to mind a newspaper article he had read about education funding in another state. The headline of the article and most of the content bemoaned the fact that that state spent much less per pupil than the national average, and the article's author thought that should be a concern for the citizens and lawmakers. Buried in the article, however, was the fact that students in that state consistently scored very high on national test scores.

Herb was familiar with that state and had friends and relatives from there. He knew, in general, people in that state valued education more highly than in his state. The system was doing a good job of educating those students, despite the funding. What mattered most when it came to how well students would perform was not how much money is spent on them, but on their attitude in school.

Herb could clearly see there was a disconnect between these parents and others in the public who saw poor school performance and assumed it was a school system problem. Poor quality teachers, lack of funding, too many students in the classroom, inept administration, etc. For those who cared, it was hard, or inconceivable, for them to see parents who would not place great value on their children's education. Thus, an objective discussion was next to impossible because focusing on the parents would make the half of parents who cared upset.

Furthermore, in the public's eye, educators placing blame on parents is an attempt to deflect the blame to someone else. Herb would admit that yes, there were teachers that could be better, but he would argue you could go to almost any business and find both good- and poor-quality employees.

He also knew the disconnect goes further. Some would point to private schools and say that they are doing a good job, "Look at how those students excel!" Critics of that argument would say that the deck was stacked in the private school's favor because they get the cream of the students, and they also attract better teachers. Some in that argument insist that providing choice to all the students and parents on where they can go to school will solve the problem of poor-quality schools because all schools will have to compete.

All these sides ignore the basic fact that it is the parents who value education most that send their children to private schools. Giving a choice to everyone, patterning programs after what one sees in private schools, or demanding greater accountability of teachers in public schools, will not change the fundamentals of parental attitude.

Herb could see all of this from where he was sitting. His big problem was what to do. He had no control over the attitude of the parents, and his position offered no authority in that direction. He also determined if he was to keep his seat on the board, he would need to walk a delicate line that did not create controversy or alienate the parents who did care, and who would most likely vote in the school board elections. Herb could see the disconnect, but he could not see how to bridge the gap.

DISCONNECTS ARE EVERYWHERE

The preceding parable illustrates a disconnect that paralyzes much meaningful progress with respect to improving education in our nation. There are plenty of statistics that indicate the United States is slipping significantly, compared to many other developed nations, with respect to child education. An objective look at those other nations finds, *on average,* they value education more highly than we in the United States.

Most people look at statistics like that and think we must be doing something wrong in our educational system. So new laws are passed to require child testing, teacher testing, or minimum teaching standards. Meanwhile, the fundamental problem of parent's attitude, which is off limits to discussion in most venues, is avoided. Boards and commissions focus on what they can influence, while fundamental problems go unaddressed for lack of an objective venue and appropriate authority.

The statistics only tell us about the average student or person or whatever is being evaluated. In the United States there are still many exceptional children, and our nation is still seen by much of the world as a land of opportunity. What is happening is we've been selectively supporting lower-income and less-educated citizens to have children, while our better educated and more affluent citizens, in general, reduce the number of children they have. Through government programs, devised with the best of intentions, we are slowly enabling and growing a class of poverty. Statistically, this results in lower average measures of academic performance, including test scores.

With this example in mind, one can step back and look at many controversial issues in the United States and find disconnects between factions. The disconnects may be due to differing perspectives, and the failure of one side, or all sides, to bother or care enough to consider what the other sides are saying. Often, both sides fail to contemplate the possibility there are alternatives neither side recognizes. You may have noticed disconnects pointed out in some of the other chapters in this book. The following are two additional brief examples of what I am talking about.

HEALTH CARE

This is a complicated issue with multiple sides. The following is just a short sampling of some of the disconnects:

- The very title of the issue creates a disconnect. The debate on this issue is really about who pays for medical procedures.
- The need for many medical procedures often results from the patient living a relatively unhealthy lifestyle.
- Having someone other than the patient providing the funding for their medical care creates a serious disconnect that removes market forces from helping to keep costs under control.
- One can lead a very healthy lifestyle and yet have no medical insurance and never see a doctor.
- A reliance on medical care to solve health issues leads many individuals to live relatively unhealthy lifestyles. This includes many in the medical field providing the care.
- Those who live an unhealthy lifestyle may receive the largest

financial benefits from the "Health Care" system because they will need a greater level of medical care to address the issues resulting from their poor health choices.

- Large entities such as governments control their costs by negotiating price limits on what they pay for medical procedures for those within their coverage. This forces the medical providers to raise their standard rates so they can afford to provide discounts. This results in higher costs overall. This is typically the net effect of price controls, overall increased prices.

Reading this list makes me think a better title for the controversy would be "Cost of Medical Coverage" rather than "Health Care." This points to one way to start to overcome a disconnect, seek to identify and focus on the real issue and avoid euphemisms.

THE DRUG WAR

We have been fighting the war on drugs for decades, and it just seems to get worse. The reason we fight this war is to protect our citizens, and particularly our children, from the availability of dangerous drugs that have detrimental and addictive effects on users. Citizens, parents, legislators, and law enforcement officers supporting and fighting this war do so believing they are helping to protect our children from the scourge of drugs.

On the other hand, most of the property and violent crime in our nation can be traced back to illegal drug use. The illicit drug trade funds, grows, and emboldens not only violent gangs, but also terrorist organizations. Further, the availability of illegal drugs on the street seems unabated.

In the face of overcrowded prisons and the unabated presence of drugs on the street, a former governor of my home state suggested several years ago we should consider the decriminalization of certain drugs. His suggestion was an effort to initiate an honest discussion of what to do about the issue. His statement was met with intense ridicule from political opponents as well as some from his own party and the general public. They were all looking at the issue from one side without listening to the reasons for his suggestion. His political opponents also saw this as an opportunity to attack a popular governor and his political party.

This is not an "either/or" issue. There are multiple sides, but at some point, with this and many other issues, society needs to stop and step back with an overall perspective and say, "This is not working. What do we need to do differently?" In this case, there are additional disconnects that complicate the "War." Efforts to aid in the fight against drug use such as drug testing, searches of lockers and offices in workplaces and schools, drug testing to receive government benefits, and other measures, have been opposed by various groups, including unions, school officials, and civil rights groups. Members of these groups no doubt include many who support the War on Drugs, but oppose actions that may be necessary to "win" that war.

This is a difficult issue that costs our society dearly. It is something I think can and must be dealt with. My brief discussion above points to another path to resolve disconnects. That is to acknowledge that disconnects exist, and that each side has a valid position that should be heard and considered to determine a best way forward. Engaging in dialog regarding a problem in a group, where parties all are intent on finding the best solutions and willing to listen and consider others, often results in the emergence of new ideas. Our failure to do this, and the tendency to be polarized in our view of the world, results in an inability to come to grips with major issues we face.

POLARIZED PERSPECTIVES

Individuals with radically different perspectives tend to self-reinforce their views while self-isolating themselves from opposing viewpoints. Many, if not most, individuals of strong polarized opinion tend to isolate themselves by associating with like-minded individuals, exposing themselves to a limited number of news information sources that favor one side and consciously or unconsciously closing their minds to differing perspectives. Furthermore, I believe that our highly advanced communication network ironically enables individuals to be more isolated.

Extended direct interpersonal discussions, which were once the primary form of communication, have been replaced by abbreviated electronic messages. The give and take of a personal conversation that can explore the various possibilities and viewpoints of an issue are reduced. Also, time spent viewing and being entertained by television, movies, video games, social media, and other internet phenomenon diminishes the time spent in meaningful conversation, intentional learning, or contemplation of ideas.

The disconnects and lack of open-minded perspective do much damage to a society. Consider the following:

- A divided society that cannot come to a common course or solution to a problem or threat will fail in providing adequate, appropriate, or timely responses to adversities that arise.
- Limited perspectives reduce the scope and range of possible options under consideration. There always exists a variety of courses one may take when addressing a circumstance. The possibilities we can envision are limited by our perspective.
- A society further limits the possibilities open to them when disconnects inhibit free discussion of a concern. Open discussions

with constructive questions bring to light new thoughts and ideas, not previously considered by any interested parties.

IMPOSITION OF PERSPECTIVE

When one opinion or perspective forcefully imposes itself upon a society, further narrowing of options and innovations occurs. As shown in the partial list below, a viewpoint can be forced upon society in many ways, escalating from subtle persuasion to extreme violence.

- Biased media coverage
- Social shaming
- Enforced censorship of converse opinions
- Economic sanctions
- Legal restrictions and prohibitions
- Criminalizing noncompliant behaviors
- Destruction of converse information (book burning, destruction of monuments, and buildings)
- Threat of physical violence, "re-education" camps
- Killing of noncompliant individuals and groups

Carried to the extreme, a great loss of knowledge and perspective occurs in a society when significant segments of history, culture, and scientific knowledge are purged. Those in power may flourish temporarily, but long term, such one-sided dominance cannot be sustained. Ultimately there will be another regime, culture, or nation that will surpass and overcome the unbalanced one-sided society.

Looking back at my list, it may seem hyperbolic, but not when put in a real-world perspective. In the last century, tens of millions of people in several different countries lost their lives to the very things listed above. All these items continue to this day in various locations in the world.

I wrote the above list in the summer of 2019. At that time, I pointed out that in the United States, we were already flirting with several items on the list. I commented that individuals isolated in their extremism become blind to the radical nature of enforcement measures that their favored faction employs. I provide the case of Colorado baker Jack Phillips as an example.

The Colorado Civil Rights Commission sought to sanction and fine Jack Phillips for refusing to decorate a cake for a same-sex marriage on the basis of his religious belief that marriage was designated by God to be between a man and a woman. A commissioner compared him to those who used religion to justify slavery and the holocaust. The case ultimately ended up in the US Supreme Court, which ruled in favor of Mr. Phillips in a 7 to 2 decision.

Under the logic being used in this case by the Commission and those of the LGBTQ community, a man who had survived the holocaust would be required to bake a cake for a neo-Nazi extremist who wanted a cake with a swastika on it. The swastika was the symbol of the Nazi regime that persecuted and killed not only Jews, but also other groups including homosexuals. The irony of this disconnect on the part of those pursuing the ruin of Jack Phillips would be laughable if the implications of it were not so serious.

Less than a year after I made the list, we witnessed the destruction of statues and buildings across our nation. Often these acts went unpunished. We have come to a very disturbing point in time. Today in the year 2021, we are very far down the list.

BEYOND REASONING

With some there is no reasoning. There is no convincing them of an alternative possibility. They are not open to engaging in a reasoned discussion. They will have some of the following traits:

- They hold an extreme point of view and see any other points of view as bigoted, unworthy, evil.
- They distort facts and/or outright lie about those who hold an opposing view. They seek to discredit the "opposition", sway others to not support or listen to the "opposition," and try to scare the "opposition" into submission to their side (see Nehemiah 6 & 7, NRSV).
- They accept anything negative about the "other side" as true, and ignore the negative that might be present in their viewpoint.
- They only listen to discussions, news, and commentaries that agree with and enforce their point of view.
- The ability to reason within them is subordinated to their emotions, anger and hatred that reinforces and fuels their bias.
- In any discussion they engage in with those who oppose them, they will seek to dominate and talk over the "opposition," thus eliminating any chance of a reasonable discussion.
- They fail to recognize that they are the epitome of what they accuse the other side to be. Such persons that read this think I am talking about those on the other side.

An objective person listening to all sides can usually discern the extremist who is intolerant of other opinions. However, this can be difficult in some cases, because there are those who will lie or be vague about their own opinions to disguise their true intentions.

ABDICATION OF POWER

It is ironic that by past actions of Congress and state legislatures, the power of the executive branches has been blown out of proportion to what is prudent. We were to the point in the last two presidencies (Obama and Trump) where the Executive unilaterally acted without direct consent of Congress. As soon as Biden took over the office, he acted with absolute impunity. This has been building for decades.

Through the years, Congress gradually abdicated and outright granted more powers to the executive branch, both to the president, as well as unelected bureaucracy. Congress has done this in many ways, including:

- In the guise of providing for immediate response to threats to national security, give the president authority to take actions in various circumstances, to spend money, and obligate forces, without prior consent of Congress. In some cases, the conditions under which such powers may be exercised are open to broad interpretation.
- Increase the number of departments and agencies in the federal government, thus expanding the scope of executive power over the lives and business of citizens.
- With each new program, grant authority to unelected executive branch bureaucrats to draft and create new regulations. Once born, these agencies are constantly adding new regulations to the tens of thousands of pages of laws and regulations we already have in the Federal Code. They become motivated by self-preservation, which can run counter to efforts to streamline and make government more efficient. Further, career bureaucrats may carry on personal agendas that oppose the policies of new administrations and the will of the electorate.

- Failing to provide proper fiscal and functional oversight over programs created, including periodic evaluation of programs that have run their course and should be eliminated.
- Failure to provide proper financial guidance and exercise fiscal restraint. For twenty years (as of this writing in 2020), Congress failed to provide a budget on time, without the use of continuing resolutions. Furthermore, a lack of restraint now creates runaway deficits, with no plan to contain out-of-control spending.

In 2019, the party opposed to that which controlled the White House virulently opposed any actions of the sitting president. Rather than rationally pursue to curtail the scope and reach of the executive branch by reasonable legislation and budget constraints, the House voted to impeach the president for doing nothing more, and perhaps less, than what his predecessors did, under the watch of many of the same Congress members who voted to impeach.

THE VOTING BOOTH

This may be the most dangerous disconnect to the future of our free republic. There is a wide disconnect among voters regarding what they want and what and for whom they vote. A vast divide exists between cause and effect when it comes to actions of government versus the livelihood and welfare of the average citizen. The effects on their lives caused by politicians are clouded by political rhetoric, opinionated media, lack of education in civics and economics, and a lost appreciation of the morals in the Christian faith that enable a free-market system to thrive.

This is a fundamental point I attempt to make throughout the pages of this book. Many citizens vote with the best of intentions, unaware they may be voting for an individual or new law that ultimately results in the opposite of what they desire for themselves, their families, and the nation.

CHAPTER 13

PANDEMIC

"Now therefore let Pharaoh select a man who is discerning and wise, and set him over the land of Egypt. Let Pharaoh proceed to appoint overseers over the land, and take one-fifth of the produce of the land of Egypt during the seven plenteous years. Let them gather all the food of these good years that are coming, and lay up grain under the authority of Pharaoh for food in the cities, and let them keep it. That food shall be a reserve for the land against the seven years of famine that are to befall the land of Egypt, so that the land may not perish through the famine."

Genesis 41:33–36 NRSV

APRIL 5, 2020

Today is April 5, 2020. As I try to complete my writing, events are rapidly unfolding. Our nation is in the tightening grip of the COVID-19 pandemic. It is interesting with all our medical knowledge how unprepared we are as a society.

The last pandemic of magnitude comparable to the potential of COVID-19 occurred one hundred years ago, from the fall of 1917 to the spring of 1919. The spread of a deadly influenza strain in the United States was aided by the gathering and transport of troops to and from the fighting of World War I in Europe. In 1918, more US troops died from influenza than they did in combat. In the United States, about 675,000 people lost their lives to the illness. With no vaccines, local governments tried to control the spread of infection using quarantines, business and school closures, wearing masks when in public, and telling people to avoid contact with others.

We face the same type of pandemic today. As of April 2020, we have no vaccine for COVID-19. The tools we possess to control the spread of the disease are the same as those available one hundred years ago. We do have better medical technologies, and antibiotics to help fight certain complications brought on by the virus. Unfortunately, we appear to be woefully unprepared both in the medical community, and as a society in general, to combat the spread and treat victims of this illness.

A week ago, I learned from my sister-in-law that my sixty-six-year-old brother had been admitted to a hospital in Seattle, because he tested positive for the coronavirus. He was admitted because he had low oxygen levels. He had been sick for a few days before testing positive, but he told me later he never really felt too bad at the time he was admitted into the hospital.

Today, I talked to my brother and learned that new test results indicated he is not doing as well as he had thought. He is still in the hospital, and he thinks he felt better the last few days because they were giving him oxygen. Meanwhile the virus was entrenching itself in his lungs. His hopes to get out of the hospital in a few days were replaced by the realization it could be many days to weeks before he could recover enough to be released.

VIRAL POLITICS

As schools and businesses closed to slow the spread of the virus, politicians around the country realized the detrimental effects such actions have on the economy. The president and members of Congress considered steps to ameliorate economic damage. Senate Republicans proposed a stimulus bill that provided for COVID-19 specific concerns, unemployment, and business assistance, and general stimulus money to be given to everyone below a specified income level. The bill consisted of hundreds of pages with a price tag of $1.8 trillion.

On March 23, Democrat House Speaker Nancy Pelosi put forth a 1,400-page alternative proposal that would cost $2.5 trillion. She stated the Republican bill was not enough. Scrutiny of the Pelosi bill found abundant additions unrelated to fighting the COVID-19, or stimulating the economy, but promoted items desired by liberals in the Democratic Party. The items included such things as mandating diversity on corporate boards, requiring airlines to reduce emissions, increasing union bargaining power, and prohibiting universities from disclosing the citizen status of their students. None of these items address problems created by the virus.

The final approved bill was a whopping $2.2 trillion. The entire concept of stimulus is political. The attempt by Nancy Pelosi to use a stimulus plan to push political agendas illustrates one problem with the stimulus concept—the great temptation to use stimulus money to promote partisan agendas. Apparently, Ms. Pelosi, and others in both parties in Congress, are familiar with this practice.

Part of the stimulus bill included sending a check to every taxpayer, regardless of whether they were affected by the virus. I heard several people indicate that sending checks to all people who file tax returns is simply returning tax money to the taxpayers. Today this is not true.

All the tax money is already spent. Every dollar of every COVID relief bill passed by Congress is deficit spending. It is borrowed or printed money, increasing the public debt and devaluing the dollar. There is no real money.

SINKING THE DOW

The reaction of the stock market to the coronavirus was dramatic. The first reaction to the potential negative effects on the economy resulted in a steady precipitous drop in all market indexes from February 20 to March 23. The Dow went from a near-record high of +29,220 to a low of 18,592. The market then rebounded just as quickly to the range of 23,000 to 24,000 on April 25, 2020.

These gyrations reveal the ephemeral nature of the apparent wealth in the stock market. In one month, the total capitalization of US stock markets lost somewhere in the range of thirteen trillion dollars. That is nearly three years of federal budgets, including mandatory spending on Social Security. It is over half the GDP for the US in 2019. How can that amount of money simply disappear in one month? In the following month, about six trillion dollars reappeared in the total of US exchanges. These are staggering sums to simply come and go on the whims of investors. Without clear positive fiscal leadership, this is a portent of things to come!

The market rebounded by news of stimulus money created by the federal government. Remember, printing money favors those with significant investments. Most of those dollars sooner or later end up in the financial markets, producing a favorable short-term outcome for stock prices. All that new money is bad for low-income families who have little or no investments, bad for all consumers who will pay higher prices, and bad for future taxpayers, our children, and grandchildren, who ultimately must pay for the debt and interest, or worse, suffer the destruction of our nation.

DEBT ADDICTION

The magnitude of the spending bills is staggering. Consider the total 2020 discretionary budget for the federal government pre-COVID was about $1.5 trillion. The first stimulus bill passed, the CARES act, was $2.3 trillion. That is $0.8 trillion or 50% more than the entire budget for all defense and domestic program spending for the year.

The projected budget deficit before the virus was $1.1 trillion. The first COVID-19 stimulus bill tripled the deficit for the year 2020, and more spending bills in the name of stimulus and fighting the virus followed. The total spending to "save" us from the coronavirus exceeds the total projected federal budget for the year.

There are some who pass off this current spending as manageable by comparing this to the deficit spending during World War II. This logic ignores the extent of extreme deficits in World War II was only four years long and was funded in part by Americans purchasing war bonds. At this present time, we have been engaged in massive deficit spending for two decades. Further, the spending for WWII had a specific end. Today the deficits are incorporated into our ongoing expenses. There is no end point established, such as the defeat and surrender of the enemy in 1945. There is no end in sight of our massive accumulation of debt.

We are locked in a pattern of falling from one crisis to the next. Each time we ratchet up the accumulation of debt with no plan to reverse the trend at the end of the crisis. The generation that fought

World War II felt a responsibility to repay the debt. Today, there is no societal sense of personal responsibility for debts we incur through spending by the federal government.

I am not opposed to a government response that involves spending money. However, it should be specifically targeted aid to those directly affected by the virus and government-ordered restrictions and closures. If crafted appropriately, the CARES bill could have cost a small fraction of its ultimate price tag.

It is absurd to believe that the response to the virus needs to cost more than the entire federal budget for the year. Competition between the two political parties kept bidding up the cost. The leadership in both parties in Congress and the Trump White House appeared to all agree with the massive spending. This will do great damage to us in the long run.

It is most concerning that after each crisis, the spending does not return to pre-crisis levels. This must stop. It requires leadership that can clearly convey the need for prudent fiscal management, and media who state facts objectively and avoid sensationalism, hyperbole, politicization, and biased agendas.

We need politicians who make objective decisions based upon what is best for the nation and avoid driving up costs by criticizing their opponents for not spending enough. Finally, we need citizens who understand the need for fiscal restraint in government and hold their representatives accountable for actions that harm the stability and security of our nation.

PRODUCTIVITY BASED RESPONSE

Thus far, I have discussed the response to COVID from the conventional knee-jerk perspective taken by politicians in Congress and the White House. Aside from the outright give away of nonexistent dollars, the current legislation subsidizes businesses to operate at a loss to keep their employees employed. There are alternatives that could make better use of capital resources and result in more efficient, market-based responses.

The current crisis is creating a new economic normal. There are new winners and losers being created. The winners are those already in position to provide their products and services delivered to people's doorsteps. Businesses such as Amazon, Instacart, Walmart, DoorDash, and Grubhub, to name a few, hired tens of thousands more employees to meet the expanding business of home-delivered shopping and dining.

The losers are those considered nonessential. They depend entirely upon customers coming into their building to buy goods or receive services. Instead of government simply shutting them down, they should have been allowed to install protections to prevent the spread of disease to customers and continue operating. Businesses have put in place many mitigating features and procedures that were relatively simple and inexpensive. In many cases, there was no need for blanket shutdowns of small businesses and restaurants.

Is it not better to provide funding to businesses to restore their productive capacity rather than just pay businesses to keep people on the payroll while operating at a loss? Using this model for economic growth would itself result in a flurry of innovation and development as tens of thousands of businesses experiment, change, learn, and grow.

The reality is there was already a major paradigm shift underway before the onset of the COVID crisis. The virus merely accelerated this shift. Rapidly developing technology enables millions of employees to work from home. Large multistory office buildings, housing hundreds or thousands of employees in enclosed spaces, are no longer necessary for many businesses.

There will always be a need or desire for face-to-face meetings, but many day-to-day business functions for office personnel can be performed from home. Work at home for millions of employees represents a significant increase in productivity. Accelerated funding and loan programs that facilitate the acquisition of the hardware and software to make such transitions clearly represent an increase in productivity.

EDUCATION PARADIGM SHIFT

Education was significantly impacted by the Coronavirus response. Nearly all schools closed in most states when the pandemic hit, but that did not mean academic education should cease. Online education has been a growing phenomenon for years.

Classes can reorganize to utilize a hybrid of online and in-class activities. This would not only reduce the potential illness-sharing interactions of students, but represents a tremendous savings in construction and maintenance of "brick and mortar" school facilities. Also, online education can be more efficient for some subjects, because one teacher, working from home, can teach a larger number of students without having to be concerned with maintaining classroom discipline. The potential productivity increase and capital funds savings are significant.

A possible objection to this hybrid education model will come from parents who both work away from the home each day. How will they supervise their children during the day? To that, I ask what do they do during the summer when children are not in school? Both these questions overlook many options if one steps out of the traditional public education box.

Some online education does not have to happen at one particular time. Pre-recorded lessons can be viewed at any time. Such lessons recorded by one teacher can be utilized by an unlimited number of students. Parents can view them with their children as they have time.

Live online lessons are necessary for some subjects. For those, there should also be some flexibility in what times those are offered. In addition, for situations where scheduling is difficult for parents, small neighborhood group cooperatives can be developed. Americans already home school an estimated 2.5 million children in our nation.[39] They have cooperative organizations that include sharing educational efforts. Their example provides a variety of solutions to the objections that may be raised to hybrid online public education.

There is a need for children to come together and interact, and there are subjects that require direct active interaction between teachers and students. Laboratory sciences, creative arts, vocational training, physical education, to name a few, need direct involvement. Savings in space and teacher's time in certain online education provides additional space and educator's time to provide live instruction in smaller and more controlled class settings.

The connectivity, mobility, and depth of readily accessible knowledge creates the potential for a much more enriching and engaging educational experience for our children. This potential can be tapped if creative market forces are enabled to participate. Education will stagnate as long as entrenched interests such as teachers' unions and political factions and agendas hold sway over the process.

This entire discussion should raise another thought for society to consider. We have become overly dependent upon families where both parents must work. I suggest it is time for parents, employers, and society in general to rethink the family-work-education paradigm.

FUTURE PRESENT PAST

The COVID-19 crisis illustrates failures of our government and society that objective examination on our part will teach lessons for the future. The importance to society of planning for the future is not a new concept. A quote at the beginning of this chapter is from Genesis Chapter 41, quoting Joseph speaking to the Pharaoh of Egypt.

Joseph was sold into slavery in Egypt. Through a series of Providential ups and downs, Joseph ended up before Pharaoh, king of Egypt. Because God enabled him to accurately interpret the king's dream, Joseph became manager of the kingdom's affairs. He prepared the nation during a time of plenty for a famine predicted by God. Joseph's God-given success resulted in the survival of the people of Israel, about 3,700 years ago. God taught us the need to predict and prepare for future crises nearly four millennia past.

The potential threat of a pandemic or a biowarfare attack on our nation is certainly not a surprise, and we should not have been so awkwardly unprepared. A nation with our technology and productive capacity should not have been caught short. The nonexistence of reserve funding to provide an immediate response to such a crisis, and the lack of domestic productive capacity to provide basic medical needs, point to a lack of foresight and economic planning on our part. There is no political party that can claim innocence in this regard.

Our unrestrained spending, with no sense of personal responsibility by politicians, or citizens, sooner or later, will lead to severe economic distress. Any plan devised to lead the nation out of the current malaise should address bringing out-of-control spending under control. The COVID crisis provided an opportunity to come together in the interest of the entire nation and correct our course. I had hoped this would be the case . . . . It was not.

CHAPTER 14

TRAGIC DECEIT

"For the hurt of my poor people I am hurt, I mourn, and dismay has taken hold of me. Is there no balm in Gilead? Is there no physician there? Why then has the health of my poor people not been restored?"

Jeremiah 8:21–22, NRSV

"Falsehood flies, and truth comes limping after it, so that when men come to be undeceived, it is too late; the jest is over, and the tale hath had its effect: like a man, who hath thought of a good repartee when the discourse is changed, or the company parted; or like a physician, who hath found out an infallible medicine, after the patient is dead."

Jonathan Swift, November 9, 1710

APRIL 25, 2020

On April 14, I called my brother as I had other times in the last two weeks. He had been in the hospital for sixteen days at that point. He did not sound well. They had him on an oxygen concentrator. He was in the middle of trying to eat, which had become difficult. We kept the conversation short, so he could get back to his meal.

On the morning of April 16, while at work, I received a call from his wife to tell me that they had transferred him to ICU, and had put him on a ventilator. That evening, I looked up the typical use of ventilators, and how they are being used against COVID-19.

A ventilator is a common tool used for treating severe cases of influenza-induced pneumonia. It buys a few days of time needed to get antibiotics into the patient's system and working to overcome the infection in the lungs. Typically, after a few days, the ventilator can be removed as the patient recovers. This is successful for most such cases.

Doctors applied this same logic to the coronavirus. Unfortunately, the virus is not the same thing. The virus attacks the lungs directly and does not respond to antibiotics. Based on what we knew at the time, most patients did not survive once they reached the point of requiring a ventilator. This was disturbing news to me. I had been led to believe from news reports that ventilators were a key component needed to save lives.

Four days later, I learned from his wife that he had developed complications in his lungs. They had done all they could for him, but his condition was failing. They kept the machine running for one more day in the hope that things would change, but they did not. He died at 6:00 p.m. on Tuesday, April 21, 2020. At that time, he was one of about 700 individuals who had succumbed to the coronavirus in King County, which has a population over 2.2 million. I wasn't sure what to think, it didn't seem real.

For most people, the coronavirus is not a life-threatening illness. Exposure to it leads to mild symptoms for some, and apparently, many suffer no symptoms at all. I am glad for them. My brother was not so fortunate.

I wondered on this day, April 25, 2020, if he would have been better off not being confined to a hospital bed, where he lay immobile, growing weaker and more dependent upon oxygen by each passing day. Would he have been better off someplace where he could get up and move around and be able to exercise his legs and lungs periodically? Is there a better model to consult for treating those with COVID symptoms without a known cure? What about how tuberculosis was treated before the advent of vaccines and antibiotics? I did not know the medical answers. I merely ask questions in hopes it might spark a useful idea that could save another life.

When my brother checked into the hospital, he anticipated that he would only be there for a few days, maybe a week. That is how we typically experience a hospital visit. After the first week, he realized it was not going to be that easy, but he was still optimistic.

He had little to do while there. He could not have visitors. All people treating him had masks covering their faces. His wife and I could only call and talk to him on his cell phone, but that ended when he went on the ventilator. We lived with the same hope he had, that he would endure the symptoms until his body's resistance caught up with the virus, and overcame it.

My last call with him was on the 14th. His last conversation with his wife was hours before he went into ICU. Neither was thought to be a final goodbye. In ICU, to insert and operate the ventilator, they place you on heavy sedation. Essentially, they put you to sleep. While on the ventilator, you remain sedated. As he was being put to sleep, he did so with every intention of waking up days later, recovering from the virus . . . . He never woke up.

MARCH 22, 2021

Today, as I pick up from where I left off writing on this subject, it has been a year since my brother became ill with the SARS-CoV-2 strain, initially called the Wuhan coronavirus, and later referred to as COVID-19. On March 19, 2020, President Donald Trump proposed the possibility of using existing drugs, including hydroxychloroquine (HCQ) to treat COVID-19. President Trump's assertion was initially based upon a French study that HCQ, in concert with Azithromycin, showed promise as an effective treatment for COVID.

The following day, Dr. Anthony Fauci, long-time director of the National Institute of Allergy and Infectious Diseases (NIAID), stated HCQ was not an effective treatment. The dominant media, in opposition to Trump, picked up on Fauci's comment, and began building a narrative that HCQ was not effective against the virus, and was even potentially dangerous.

As this narrative grew, it had the effect of muting medical practitioners treating COVID patients who experienced first-hand the efficacy of utilizing HCQ, particularly in combination with other substances. Following the narrative, hospitals, insurance companies, other corporate medical entities, and even governments, instructed doctors to not use HCQ.

On April 1, 2020, Rudy Giuliani, in Episode 21 of his online series Common Sense, interviewed Dr. Vladimir Zelenko. Dr. Zelenko, is a general practice physician for the village of Kiryas Joel, a Hasidic Jewish community an hour drive north of New York City. He described a treatment for COVID-19 he developed based upon the French study Trump referenced, together with a Korean study that combined HCQ with zinc. He had researched each ingredient of his medicinal "cocktail," and explained in clear language how they combined to form an effective treatment for COVID-19 patients. He included specific dosages of each of the three ingredients, HCQ, zinc, and Azithromycin.

Dr. Zelenko further explained the application of the "cocktail" therapy. It could be dispensed to outpatients, and should be given as close to onset as practical. Hospitalization should be avoided. It was not anticipated as an effective treatment once the virus has progressed to the point that it would require a ventilator. The indications for prescribing the "cocktail" included individuals over sixty years of age, and others who had chronic health conditions or had a compromised immune system. He did not routinely prescribe his treatment for healthy individuals under sixty years of age. At the time of the interview, although he had only begun the therapy a week earlier, he had treated hundreds of patients, with no deaths.

It was well established that zinc in cells under viral attack interrupts replication of the virus. Zinc does not adsorb well, but the addition of HCQ facilitates the introduction of zinc into the cells. The combination of HCQ and zinc, given over a five-day period, gives the patient's immune system time to react to the virus before the virus can inflict serious lung damage. The Azithromycin simply protects against complicating infections that might develop from a compromised immune system.

The small-town family practitioner, from his home in Kiryas Joel, had researched potential treatments for COVID-19. He arrived on a viable drug therapy supported by established science, using readily available components that had been in use for decades with few complications. The components of his five-day "cocktail" therapy had an estimated cost of about twenty dollars.

That interview took place just a couple of days after my brother was admitted into the hospital, when he still did not feel too bad, and had not yet begun to develop the complication that ultimately took his life.

After a week of being bed ridden, not because he felt bad, but because he was told he should check into the hospital, blood clots began to form in his legs. After about another week and a half, blood clots began to form in his lungs. I was able to talk to the doctor treating him in the hospital the day before my brother passed away. He explained they could fight the virus alone, and they could treat blood clotting, but the two combined were overwhelming.

I did not learn about and view the video of Dr. Zelenko until today, March 22, 2021. Why was this not in the dominant national news networks? Why the suppression of a viable therapy that had the potential to enable those most susceptible to survive the deadly nature of the virus? At the time of my brother's death, I questioned if there were other treatment options. It is clear to me now, there were.

THE GREAT SUPPRESSION

Instead of collective reason, the reaction to HCQ was turned into an instant political controversy that was used to discredit President Trump. Media giants and some government bureaucrats were quick to point to quotes of medical professionals that were critical of the promotion of HCQ, and publicized studies that indicated HCQ by itself was not effective against the virus. Criticism of HCQ and Trump were often linked together in the same articles.

One such article was an opinion written by the Editorial Board of the *Washington Post* on April 23, 2020. The article refers to the French study. It also cites a small preliminary retrospective study of patients at a Veterans Affairs facility that found HCQ did not help, and possibly made things worse. Finally, it referenced a statement by a panel of US government agencies and medical associations recommending against the use of HCQ. No mention of Dr. Zelenko's work, which by then should have been known to any professional in the medical and media fields making a sincere and unbiased search for answers to treat the virus.

The opinion went on to state, "The United States has built a process of drug testing and approvals considered the gold standard around the world, involving three phases of clinical trials to test safety, dosage, efficacy, and possible side effects of a new drug or vaccine. The fear inspired by the coronavirus must not undermine this rigorous procedure."[40] HCQ, zinc, and Azithromycin were not new drugs. They had been available and approved safe for use by the US government for decades. General claims that HCQ was dangerous were simply false.

Parallel to the anti-HCQ narrative were other notable media biases.

- There was constant daily coverage of the death toll due to COVID that stoked the fear factor. This coverage was often decoupled from the age and pre-existing health conditions of the victims. Note that eighty percent of victims of COVID in 2020 were sixty-five and older, most with pre-existing or weakened health conditions.
- Coverage focused on the number of reported cases by positive test results, and the death toll. This made the fatality rate appear much larger than reality. A study conducted in Santa Clara County testing for presence of COVID antibodies in the general populace, released in mid-April 2020, showed an infection rate in the population to be fifty times higher than case numbers indicated.[41]
- Rather than taking precautions to protect elderly citizens from exposure, while allowing the rest of society to remain functioning, the justification was built to close down businesses and other activities.

- Vaccines were promoted as the only real medical solution to the virus.

On October 12, 2020, a peer-reviewed study was published that stated the CDC inappropriately, and allegedly illegally, changed the criteria used in determining the cause of death in a manner that significantly increased reported COVID fatality rates.[42] The study compared what COVID death statistics would be using well-established CDC guidelines, in use for the last seventeen years, to what was being reported by the CDC, using new guidelines unilaterally issued by the CDC on March 24, 2020.

As of August 23, 2020, using the new guideline, the CDC reported 161,392 deaths due to COVID-19. According to the study, if the standard practice of reporting for the last seventeen years had been used, that total would have only been 9,684. Thus, the CDC had manipulated the way deaths were reported, possibly increasing by sixteen times, the death toll due to COVID.

On December 11, 2020, the USFDA issued an emergency use authorization for a COVID vaccine developed by Pfizer-BioNTech. The vaccine uses an mRNA technology that had not been used before in a vaccine. The emergency approval short circuits the gold standard testing that editors at the Washington Post insisted was required for any drug or vaccine promoted for use against COVID-19. There has been no time to develop an understanding of the potential long-term effects of the vaccines, but there was now a push to vaccinate all adults regardless of age, health, or existing immunity.

In March 2021, individuals who contracted and recovered from the virus were told they should receive at least one dose of the vaccine. Why? This makes no scientific sense. Those pushing this said we do not know how long immunity lasts from contracting the virus. To the contrary, we have longer duration data on natural immunity than we do for the vaccine. Existing antibody test data, that extends at least eight months, shows lasting immunity in ninety percent of those who have had COVID.[43] Further, all those people have shown their immune systems can overcome the virus. This also ignores those who have experienced the disease asymptomatically.

In my home state of New Mexico, at the end of March 2021, a media blitz was launched to encourage every "adult" (16 and older) to get vaccinated. On March 31, the announcements included the news that the Pfizer-BioNTech vaccine was seeking authorization for children down to the age of twelve years. The inoculation was now being pushed to children as well as adults, with the comment that this is the only way to defeat the virus. This despite indications that children are not significant spreaders of the virus.

Further, we have collected no data in the state that tells us about existing immunity that likely developed in the younger population. As of March 20, 2021, there had been only one death reported in New Mexico related to COVID of individuals aged seventeen and under, and that child had significant pre-existing health issues. Seroprevalence testing of children in Mississippi,[44] as well as other studies, show the presence of antibodies to the virus can be present in individuals at a rate at least ten times the virus case incidence rate. As of March 30, 2021, in New Mexico, there were 191,377 positive tests for COVID-19. The state has a population of just over two million. This would suggest there could be a significant proportion of the population that has already developed natural immunity to the virus.

Why do we not test people first to see if they already have antibody immunity in their system before subjecting them to an experimental inoculation? Congress and the president are spending trillions of nonexistent dollars on all manner of things unrelated to the pandemic under the guise of COVID-19 recovery. A tiny fraction of such money spent on widespread seroprevalence (antibody) testing would provide invaluable data about the actual spread of COVID, as well as viruses in general. It would likely show that a much larger portion of the population has immunity than the case count shows.

The CDC modified death reporting for COVID in a manner that likely resulted in an overestimate of deaths by an order of magnitude. The incidence of COVID cases appears from seroprevalence testing to underestimate the total number of individuals who contracted the virus by potentially an order of magnitude. Those two numbers are now being used to justify the never-used before vaccine technology to inoculate everyone including children. Why!?

Why subject healthy children and young adults to this experimental vaccine? In the United States, people from ages one to thirty-four are in greater danger of being a homicide victim,[45] than of dying from the Wuhan coronavirus.

I am not opposed to vaccines. It seems appropriate for those who are elderly, or have other high-risk conditions, to receive the COVID-19 inoculation. The promise of mRNA technology has the potential to create immunity in a new way that can be developed and produced in a relatively short time. It may very well be that the vaccines that have been developed are perfectly safe, have no long-term effects, and represent a new medical breakthrough. But we have no long-term testing to prove this. The drug companies have been granted immunity from liability for the vaccines. Why inoculate our children with this?

THE TRAGEDY

On January 26, 2021, a paper was published in The American Journal of Medicine authored by twenty-one doctors and two other medical professionals endorsing the use of HCQ, zinc, and Azithromycin for the early outpatient treatment of COVID-19. The indications and protocols cited in the paper follow closely those provided ten months earlier by Dr. Zelenko.

If my brother had been a patient of Dr. Zelenko, he would not have been admitted into a hospital. He would have immediately been given the five-day "cocktail" therapy and gone home. He would have remained ambulatory, moving about, perhaps preventing the formation of clots in his legs that would then spread into his lungs. His immune system would have had time to build an immunity before the virus could cause serious damage to his lungs. He could possibly be alive today.

How many others could have been saved? A small-town doctor figured this out on his own from existing data. He was motivated to do so out of sincere love and concern for his patients. What is the motivation to suppress such potential good news? In the face of a pandemic with no known cure, scientific reason would indicate the development of a clearinghouse by the NIH to track, support, and disseminate the results of frontline doctors treating the illness. It appears the opposite took place.

Rather than immediately begin studies to confirm the efficacy of the HCQ-zinc therapy, a campaign was initiated to discredit HCQ, avoid the zinc component, and then use that to discredit President Trump. At the same time, the idea that we would collectively develop immunity to the virus naturally was discredited, instead stressing the need to isolate people of all ages until a vaccine became available. The death statistics were amplified and manipulated to create an undue fear of the illness, which was then used to impose draconian social restrictions on businesses, and social and religious gatherings.

The death statistics and a deceptive media campaign created a fervent urgency for a vaccine. While rational medical answers were ignored, a twenty-billion-dollar windfall for major pharmaceutical companies was created. A special approval criterion developed by the FDA for a vaccine enabled an emergency authorization, not an approval, to use the drug, much sooner than under normal circumstances. In the meantime, people were being hospitalized, and dying, unnecessarily because existing viable alternatives, such as HCQ and zinc, had been intentionally suppressed.

A clear effort occurred to conceal potentially beneficial facts, while intentionally manipulating data, making the Wuhan coronavirus appear even more dangerous than it is. This effort included the dominant media, major medical corporations, government bureaucrats, and politicians opposed to the president. The cost of this deceit in terms of lost production and wages due to shutdowns, hospitalizations, and wasteful government spending is in the trillions of dollars. The cost in terms of lost lives, is incalculable. Consider such people that are willing to engage in a deceit that is so damaging and deadly. What won't they be willing to do?

That brings me to one more major media bias regarding COVID. About the time my brother contracted the coronavirus, a media campaign began pushing for widespread unrestricted mail-in voting, and removal of mail-in ballot security measures, for the upcoming 2020 elections. These measures were argued to be justified by a deadly pandemic that would put people at risk if they went to the polls. We were being primed to accept a vastly larger deceit, designed to destroy our republic and subvert the rights and freedoms of Americans.

CHAPTER 15

ELECTION

"Let each citizen remember at the moment he is offering his vote that he is not making a present or a compliment to please an individual – or at least that he ought not so to do; but that he is executing one of the most solemn trusts in human society for which he is accountable to God and his country."

Samuel Johnson, 1781

JANUARY 2021

While I witnessed the events unfold in the last two and a half months, some of the warnings I wrote years ago appeared prophetic. My prior writing was done in the hope of preserving our nation. The present events indicate a realization of many of the fears I warned of. We may be witnessing our rapid demise as the beacon of hope and freedom to the world. I pray that is not the case.

As I write this, our nation's capital undergoes an unprecedented militarization with a look reminiscent of former communist Eastern Europe. Barrier walls, military roadblocks, checkpoints, concertina wire, these are not scenes of a United States about to celebrate the inauguration of a new president. Plans for the inauguration called for a troop strength equivalent to two army divisions!

What has happened to our nation? Every concerned American viewing these scenes, regardless of their political persuasion, should be asking themselves this question and seeking to find answers. It is instructive to consider some historical facts.

OBAMA YEARS

During Barack Obama's tenure as president, he marshalled all resources available to him to enforce his progressive political agenda. In 2012 he used the Department of Justice to file suits in several states claiming voter ID laws discriminated against minorities because they were less likely to have an ID. The suits argued that the discrimination violated Constitutional protections against voter discrimination, insinuating ID laws are intentionally racist. Republicans countered no, the laws are a necessary part of a free voting process that protect against voter fraud, and that the suits represent attempts to enable fraud.

Following reelection in 2013, President Obama created a 501(c) (4) entity Organizing for Action, using personnel that came from his campaign organization. The organization trained activists to promote the Obama agenda. In 2019, that organization merged with the National Redistricting Action Fund (NRAF), led by Eric Holder, the former Attorney General under Obama, to become All on the Line. Their purpose is to train activists to influence the relocation of voting district boundaries. Their plan targets ten states: Florida, Georgia, North Carolina, Pennsylvania, Ohio, Michigan, Wisconsin, Colorado, Arizona, and Texas. These are the so-called swing states that, if carried, ensure a presidential victory.

While Obama built his apparatus to extend his influence over the federal government beyond his eight years in office, then Vice

President Joe Biden became the point man for the administration in other nations, including China and Ukraine. At the same time, Joe Biden's son, Hunter, made contacts and developed very lucrative business deals in both those nations. Joe Biden promoted a cooperative, and conciliatory, relationship with China. In Ukraine, he used the promise of financial aid to influence its internal affairs that suffered from corruption, political unrest, and military incursions by Russia.

In the final months of Obama's presidency, the 2016 election pitted Secretary of State and former First Lady Hillary Clinton against political outsider Donald Trump. On July 31, 2016, ten days after Trump received the Republican nomination for president, the FBI initiated a covert surveillance operation labeled Crossfire Hurricane. The agency used a document, prepared by foreign agent Christopher Steele, and funded by the Clinton campaign, as evidence to get warrants from the FISA court to surveil individuals connected with Trump's campaign. FBI officials promoted the premise there was evidence of collusion between the Trump campaign and Russia.

By all measures, Donald Trump was not supposed to win the election in 2016. Before he won the Republican nomination, there were pundits and professors floating the possibility of a Trump impeachment if he got elected.[46] Hillary Clinton had the endorsement of two popular two-term presidents, her husband Bill Clinton, and then-president Barack Obama. As a Democrat, she was the favored candidate of the dominant media. Polls indicated she had the advantage.

Despite this, at the end of the night on November 8, 2016, it was clear Donald Trump garnered a majority of electors, and in the early morning hours of November 9, Hillary Clinton called Donald Trump to concede the election. Later in the morning, she spoke publicly to her supporters stating, "Last night, I congratulated Donald Trump and offered to work with him on behalf of our country." She also said,

"Donald Trump is going to be our president. We owe him an open mind and the chance to lead."

Immediately after the election, opponents claimed the Trump presidency was illegitimate, and he was guilty of impeachable offenses. On the day of Trump's inauguration, January 20, 2017, The Washington Post ran a headline article, "The campaign to impeach President Trump has begun."[47] The article points out that while Trump was being inaugurated, a new website, ImpeachDonaldTrumpNow.org, went online. The article also stated that Democrats and liberal activist groups such as the ACLU "are mounting broad opposition to stymie Trump's agenda."

Before Trump took his first action as president, the effort to impeach him was underway. So much for open minds and providing a chance to lead.

TRUMP TIME

Several individuals in the FBI and DOJ involved with the covert Trump campaign surveillance, remained in their positions at the beginning of Trump's term. On May 17, 2017, Robert Mueller was appointed as special counsel to investigate allegations of Russian collusion with Trump. After three years of investigation, and continuous claims by the press and Democrats that proof existed of Trump's collusion, the Muller investigation concluded they could find no evidence of collusion.

While the Muller investigation dragged on, independent watchdog organizations uncovered evidence of how the Obama Administration initiated the investigation.[48] The Steele document contained unverifiable and questionable information. It was illegally doctored before being presented to the FISA court, and the questionable nature of the document was withheld from the FISA court. Personal bias was revealed on the part of FBI officials initiating the investigation, who privately expressed an intent to prevent Trump from being elected. To top it off, the document that formed the basis for the investigation was funded by the Clinton campaign. The above facts were slowly pried out of the DOJ by multiple FOIA requests. When building a legal case, the aggregate of evidence often results in a conviction, not isolated facts. While one may discount a fact in isolation, the aggregate of facts and circumstances paint a clear picture of intentional efforts to usurp the Trump campaign and presidency. The media opposed to Trump, ignored, discredited, or spun the facts, and then used the precedent of "discrediting" some evidence to categorically deny a spy operation had been undertaken against Trump.[49]

After the Muller report found no evidence of an impeachable offense, Democrats devised an alternative reason to impeach the president using a phone call by Trump to the president of Ukraine. Some administration officials claimed Trump withheld aid to Ukraine to coerce the Ukrainians to investigate former Vice President Biden. The accusation against Biden by Trump was that in March of 2016, Biden used a threat to withhold a $1 billion aid package from Ukraine if they did not remove their Prosecutor General Viktor Shokin. Shokin at the time was investigating Barisma, an energy company that paid the vice president's son Hunter Biden, and his partner, considerable sums of money for legal fees. During the time in question in 2014 and 2015, Hunter and his partner were paid fees by Barisma of about three million dollars.[50]

Thus, the Democrats accused President Trump of something similar or lesser than what Vice President Biden did more than three years prior. Trump was impeached by the House in rushed proceedings in December 2019, and acquitted by the Senate in February 2020.

While Congress distracted itself with the politics of impeachment, the Wuhan coronavirus was quickly spreading from China around the world. China also continued the methodical expansion of its military, economic, and political influence throughout the world, in particular against the United States of America.

SETTING THE ELECTION STAGE

During the year leading up to the 2020 election, both Republicans and Democrats filed suits in various states regarding election administration. Republicans focused on fraud prevention, calling for removal of dead, alien, and relocated individuals from voting rolls, and compliance with existing laws limiting mail-in ballots. Democrats opposed efforts to enforce existing laws and resisted cleaning voter rolls, arguing some voters might be disenfranchised.

Beginning in March 2020, as shutdowns due to the pandemic spread across the nation, a push started, primarily by Democrats, for universal mail-in ballots. Decisions in some states were made by election officials or judges to ease requirements for mail-in ballots, so people could avoid in-person voting. Deadlines for mail-in ballots were extended, signature matching was waived, and some states mailed ballots to all registered voters.

As an example of the jockeying that took place, consider events in Pennsylvania. In April 2020, a suit filed by a conservative-leaning organization asked that voter rolls be cleaned in Pennsylvania. The suit indicated 800,000 voter registrations might be questionable. Pennsylvania election officials countered that their rolls were in compliance, and questioned the validity of the plaintiff's claims. The judge deferred the case stating it was too close to the election. An attorney for the ACLU, siding with the state, commented regarding potential fraud, "the would-be fraudster would have to forge a signature, and would face stiff penalties if caught."[51]

Closer to election day, two issues brought up by election officials ended up before the Pennsylvania Supreme Court. On September 17, the court ruled in favor of a request to extend the deadline for receiving mail-in ballots after election day. On October 23, the court again sided with state election officials, stating that signature verification was not required on mail-in ballots.

State election officials argued the anticipated increase in mail-in ballots as justification for the extension. They ignored the fact that earlier in the year, the Republican legislature passed new legislation to allow no-excuse mail-in voting, giving state officials months to prepare for a general election with expanded mail-in voting. Further, the critical element cited earlier in the year by the ACLU lawyer as the deterrent to mail-in voter fraud, a valid signature, was removed by a state supreme court decision just eleven days before the election.

In various states, leading up to the election, Democrats argued and sued to prevent the removal of illegal aliens, dead persons, and non-residents from voter rolls. They also pushed to remove voter ID, and signature verification. These are recognized by nearly all other developed democratic nations in the world as reasonable measures to protect against voter fraud.[52] Given the actions taken by Democrat officials in swing states to subvert state laws enacted to protect against fraud, together with continuous efforts to usurp his presidency in the previous four years, President Trump had good reason to suspect improper activity in the 2020 election.

WHERE IS THE EVIDENCE?

Sometime early on the morning of November 4, 2020, President Trump declared that there was fraudulent activity taking place in the election in certain states. In the following two months, multiple suits were filed, challenging election results. Some state legislators also held hearings to receive evidence of fraud presented by Trump attorneys.

It is clear to me from what I have seen and read of the presidential vote results that irregularities in the vote count exist of sufficient magnitude to potentially affect the outcome of the elections.[53] I watched videos of interviews and read statements by affiants who testify to abundant fraudulent activities in several states. The evidence convinced me that the result of the election was far from certain, and that a thorough investigation into the attested to activities was warranted.

Democrats and their media allies denied the fraud. They asked, "Where is the evidence?" while they discredited those who came forward with eyewitness and expert testimony. They often pointed to the dismissal of multiple court cases, claiming that showed there was no fraud. This claim is misleading. Nearly all the suits in question were dismissed for administrative reasons. Often judges ruled those filing did not have standing, or the filings were not timely. Those cases were dismissed without consideration of the merits.

Further, not all cases were thrown out. For example, a case in Antrim County, Michigan, gave the plaintiff's experts access to the election machines and related storage devices used in the county. Their report became public on December 14, 2020. The report concluded that the Dominion voting machines used in the election were programmed to generate a ballot error rate sixty-eight percent of the time, causing them to be sent to adjudication.

The voting hardware and software being used can be enabled to allow someone to remotely alter the vote cast on an adjudicated ballot. The results initially reported by the county favored Biden by about 3000 votes in a strongly Republican county. A hand recount showed that Trump prevailed in the county, garnering 9,747 votes out of 15,707 total votes cast. The Michigan Secretary of State explained the mysterious vote switch was due to human error. The attorney for the plaintiff countered that the switching of votes is explained by the findings of their experts of fraudulent manipulation, not human error.

There are cases of fraud in several states that were just finally being heard in March 2021, regarding fraudulent activities from the 2020 primaries and even from the 2018 election. Contentious legal battles tend to move slowly through the judicial process. Evidence of fraud in the 2020 general election continues to accumulate, and investigations are ongoing. Using case dismissals as proof that there was no fraud in the election is deceptive and simply not valid.

MEDIA DECEPTION

Another source often pointed to by those arguing there was no fraud in the election is the preliminary report of the Electoral Observation Mission (EOM) sponsored by the Organization of American States (OAS).[54] Their report issued on November 6, 2020, included the statement that they had "not directly observed any serious irregularities that call into question the results so far." We should take note of a few things in this report.

First, the mission consisted of twenty-eight individuals who were spread between Georgia, Iowa, Maryland, Michigan, and Washington, DC. There are a total of 365 counties in the four states under observation. They were clearly spread thin on election day. Further, the nature of the alleged fraud may not be readily seen by an observer simply watching the process of voters voting and ballots being tallied. No one from the OAS was present at the State Farm Arena in Atlanta, Georgia, the night of the election, when ballot tabulation resumed after observers were told counting had stopped for the night, the work in progress had been put away, and most of the workers had left. They also were not present in Arizona, Wisconsin, Pennsylvania, or Nevada.

Second, the report discusses the media coverage. They shared concerns about the strong influence of social media companies, and how they flagged or deleted messages from certain candidates, which the report stated "is far from ideal." The report also commented that "media outlets overwhelmingly publicly endorsed the democratic candidate."

The clear media bias and a coordinated effort to influence the election was affirmed by an article published by *Time Magazine* in February 2021.[55] The article discloses Democrat's concerted efforts to control the traditional and social media narratives. They also heavily influenced regulatory decisions and intimidated government officials to prevent a Trump victory. Both the OAS-EOM report, as well as the *Time* article, show the intentional work by traditional and social media companies to bury or discredit stories unfavorable to Biden, while promoting stories unfavorable to Trump.

A conservative watchdog organization, Media Research Center, released a survey on November 24, 2020, that polled voters for Biden.[56] The survey presented to voters several news items favorable to Trump. They asked in each case if the voter knew of the news before voting, and then asked those who didn't if they would have changed their vote if they had known. The stories included such things as the US achieving energy independence, sexual assault allegations against Biden, Biden family ties to a company with Chinese Communist Party connections worth tens of millions of dollars to the Bidens, and the landmark Middle East peace agreements brokered by the Trump administration.

The percent of Biden voters unaware of the stories ranged from eighteen to fifty-one percent, depending upon the issue. Typically, seventy-five to eighty-five percent of those unaware said they would not have changed their vote. The majority of the remaining said that they would not have voted for Biden had they known of some of these items. The numbers suggest that, in the absence of information suppression, possibly one to two percent of Biden voters might have switched to Trump, and an additional three to six percent of Biden voters would have chosen a third-party candidate or simply not have voted for president.

If one simply takes three percent of votes away from Biden in four states, Trump would have won in Arizona, Wisconsin, Pennsylvania, and Georgia. This would have given Trump enough electoral votes to win the election. Media bias clearly influenced voters on a scale large enough to potentially change the outcome of the election.

The *Time Magazine* article portrays the outcome of the biased effort as cause to celebrate. This demonstrates a clear, intentional bias. For individuals and entities that are subject to US communication, campaign, and tax regulations, this could represent violations of federal laws. The clear bias flirts with violation of FCC rules governing equal access. Additionally, they may represent possible campaign finance violations that treat in-kind donations the same as cash contributions. It is appalling that so many in media, and society in general, have wandered so far from understanding the need for news agencies to provide accurate, unbiased information, even if that news is not favorable to their personal political persuasions.

ELECTION FRAUD

An HBO documentary released before the 2020 election titled *Kill Chain*, shows how vulnerable US voting machinery is to cyber manipulation. Individuals from both sides of the political aisle, as well as technology experts, are featured in the film. It points out both Russia and China have been active in compromising efforts in our elections. Evidence of manipulation in the 2016 election is included in the video.

Months after the election, evidence indicates that what was discussed in the HBO documentary appears to have occurred on a large scale in 2020. The alleged criminal manipulation of the voting system is enabled to occur by 1) widespread use of online-networked computerized vote tabulation hardware and software, 2) voter rolls with abundant non-voting registrants, 3) unrestricted mail-in ballots, 4) removal of voter ID verification and signature matching, and 5) delay of receipt and counting of mail-in ballots after election day that enables interim knowledge of the vote count by those seeking to manipulate the vote before the counting is completed.

All these required elements were pushed to be in place predominantly by Democrat election officials and operatives in key states prior to the election. Arguments most often used to justify steps that remove security in the election process are preventing disenfranchisement and racism. The rights of free citizens come with responsibilities. Providing your proof of identity to ensure election integrity is a reasonable expectation of responsible citizens. There is nothing racist about ensuring the integrity of an election. People of all races and political persuasions should want to ensure the integrity of our elections. What is racist is using race as an excuse to enable cover for criminal activity.

All those favoring the designated winner Joe Biden, chose to ignore the anomalies and move forward as if nothing was amiss. It is most disturbing that not just Democrats, but large corporate media and tech companies claimed, and continue to claim, the concerns raised by the Trump campaign are false and have no evidence supporting them. There is copious evidence,[57] [58] [59] [60] and to claim otherwise is a lie.

When did eyewitness and expert testimony with sworn affidavits by hundreds of individuals, who willingly appear in public hearings, exposing themselves to personal attacks, threats, and persecution, cease to be evidence in the United States of America? There was and continues to be a serious effort to block and hinder efforts to conduct actual audits of the ballots and machines that could definitively prove whether fraud has occurred. This effort lends great weight to suspicions that the election was fraudulently manipulated.

Only those who are party to corruption, who seek to hide their crimes, have cause to deny an honest and open accounting of votes. The magnitude and level of the alleged fraud is vast and suggests a coordinated effort across states and nations. Individuals who would undertake such actions will do anything to avoid prosecution—anything! This raises a frightening situation. It is very disconcerting that people who have come forward with evidence, and others who have represented them, have come under severe intimidation and threats of violence.

The call by President Joe Biden before and after his inauguration for the nation to come together in unity, while ignoring clear discrepancies in the vote, is disingenuous. If he believed we had an uncorrupted election, and truly sought unity, he should have been the first to call for a thorough investigation of the election. Failure to investigate only results in greater division. As Jesus taught us, "If a kingdom is divided against itself, that kingdom cannot stand."[61] Furthermore, if the election apparatus has been compromised by a single party, and that ability to compromise remains intact, then tyranny has already come upon us.

CHAPTER 16

THE FRUITS OF TYRANNY

"But false prophets also arose among the people, just as there will be false teachers among you, who will secretly bring in destructive opinions. They will even deny the Master who bought them—bringing swift destruction on themselves. Even so, many will follow their licentious ways, and because of these teachers the way of truth will be maligned. And in their greed they will exploit you with deceptive words."

2 Peter 2:1–3a, NRSV

"The accumulation of all powers, legislative, executive, and judiciary, in the same hands, whether of one, a few, or many, and whether hereditary, self-appointed, or elective, may justly be pronounced the very definition of tyranny."

James Madison, 1788

TYRANNICAL FRUITS

In the first chapter of this book, I mentioned how Jesus talked about discerning the good from the bad by examining the fruits they produce. This quote of Jesus came near the end of his "sermon on the mount."

Former President Harry Truman, once stated that he believed that there was no problem that could not be solved if approached considering the teachings of the "sermon on the mount."

When I began to put this book together, I had hoped to maintain a balanced approach. I see faults in both dominant parties. However, in the months preceding and following the 2020 presidential election, the Democrat Party, and the entities that support their agenda, demonstrated a clear abandonment of the principles essential to a free and thriving nation. The founders warned us the very existence of political parties creates an opening for tyranny to take hold. The tyrannical fruits of Democrats and their enabling patrons and media are now clear to see.

ENABLING TYRANNY

Many things I discuss in this book reflect a slow, gradual escalation of the elements of tyranny within our nation. This has taken place over the course of many years. Some of these elements include:

- Moving from self-reliance and personal responsibility to government providing for personal needs and wants.
- Congress and legislatures turning responsibilities over to executives and bureaucrats.
- Treating government authorities like monarchs, instead of accountable public servants.
- Trading productive capacity, innovative spirit, and collective wealth for personal contentment, convenience, low-cost consumer goods, and government entitlements.
- Allowing greed and avarice to lead us to trade extensively with

China, while they commit persecution and genocide against religious groups, and use our wealth and technology to build a comprehensive offensive military infrastructure, intended to be used against us.

- Failing to contain excessive spending at all levels that incurs an insurmountable debt that can cause absolute economic ruin of our nation.

- Ceding portions of our education system to factions that teach false narratives regarding our national history, and disregard economics and civics, including an appreciation for the founding documents of our nation, and the source of our prosperity.

- Creation of a large federal bureaucracy that hosts a cadre of individuals promoting a one-sided political agenda, rather than follow the role of public servant working to perform duties called for by duly enacted legislation applied equally to all citizens.

- Conversion of federal justice department agencies from apolitical entities upholding the laws of our nation, to corrupted organizations enforcing the will a single political party.

- Politicians and intellectuals espousing hyperbolic and false narratives that breeds division, violence, distrust, and makes enemies out of fellow citizens.

- Using political party affiliation to attain power rather than to achieve noble goals for the good of all.

- Abandoning the moral guiding principles of the Christian faith, and persecuting those who remain true to that faith.

For tyranny to succeed, would-be tyrants must control the nation's communication network. Today we have a media industry that evolved in part due to a self-isolating elitist educational system that channels most aspiring journalists into a one-sided political perspective. That evolution is strongly shaped by the development of new communication technologies controlled by a few individuals sharing a common political perspective. This creates monopolistic control of the dominant communication systems favoring the Democratic Party.

Censorship by traditional and social media had been ongoing before the election, but after the events of January 6, 2021 at the Capitol, widespread overt censorship began in earnest. Merely discussing evidence of election fraud was twisted into inciting violence and justification for being censored. The complicit media parroted the Democrat narrative, characterizing the events of January 6 as an attempted coup and insurrection.

CAPITOL AGGRESSION

What happened inside the Capitol Building was clearly wrong. Vandalism and theft should not be tolerated as a part of any protest, not just in the Capitol, but anywhere. Individuals who engaged in such behavior should be prosecuted. I see nothing in what Donald Trump said that would suggest he wanted or would endorse such activity.

There were many kinds of people who entered the Capitol Building that afternoon. There appeared to be many fringe individuals who behaved like fools and idiots. Others, sincerely concerned about the validity of the election, entered possibly thinking they might be able to voice their concerns directly to members of Congress.

There were others who entered with more malicious intent. Not all were Trump supporters. One prominent example was John Sullivan, an opportunistic anarchist who made a video of the event that included the shooting of Ashli Babbitt. Days before the event he posted on social media, "Time to kick this fascist out of DC on January 6, 2020. Trump is not our president dump him for good location Washington Monument 11:00 AM visit www.insurgenceusa.com for more information." On January 2, 2021, that post had seventy "likes."

Mr. Sullivan has a past record of arrest for being involved in a violent BLM protest, and has a website and media posts that promote anarchist revolutionary activities. He appeared on CNN news the evening of January 6, and was paid $70,000 by CNN and NBC for video footage he shot while in the Capitol Building.

In his video, Sullivan encourages protesters to move forward and revels in the accomplishment of successfully breaching the Capitol Building. After wandering in the building for a while, and disobeying orders from police to exit, he arrives at a barricaded interior glass doorway. Two uniformed officers and an official in a suit guard the door. Behind him, on his left, is a crowd of protesters extending back along a hallway. Behind to the right, in a stairway going down, stands a squad of well-armed riot police.

Over the noise of the crowd, Mr. Sullivan convinces the police officers to move aside. The three move right, with the riot police behind them, and Ashli Babbitt next to them. Sullivan looks forward through the glass to see a handheld gun emerge from the left. Ashli Babbitt started climbing through an opening on the right. The official holding the gun on the left side stepped forward and shot her when she was halfway through the opening. Had the shooter missed low and to his right, he may have hit one of the many police officers standing behind her.

Contrary to news reports of multiple deaths due to rioting, used to justify the impeachment of Donald Trump, Ashli Babbitt was the only death due to violence. There was only one shot fired that day. The riotous behavior by some of the few hundred individuals inside the Capitol Building on January 6, 2021, contrasts sharply with the peaceful behavior of the one hundred thousand or so pro-Trump supporters who attended the rally at the Ellipse.

Nancy Pelosi and others described what happened as an attempted coup, and labeled those present as insurrectionists. Had the hundred thousand Trump supporters who attended the rally come armed with the intention of a violent insurrection, there is nothing the Capitol Police could have done to stop them.

Some videos and photos of scenes around and within the Capitol Building show protesters breaking windows, yelling at and struggling with police at barricades, and committing acts of vandalism and theft. But other videos show police allowing protesters access, and individuals wandering inside taking photos and videos, posing for pictures, including with police officers, like a group of tourists. It is clear some entered with malicious intent, but just as clearly, others entered with no violent intent.

My reading of the president's speech appears more wistful than anything. Several times he referred to Vice President Pence, hoping that Pence would claim authority to not accept certain state's electors, even though Pence had previously indicated he would not do that. Trump stated early in his talk that the gathering at the Capitol was to be peaceful.

The last thing Republicans wanted was interference with the proceedings in the Capitol Building. The plan for Republicans was clear. Following well-established rules, they would raise objections to electors from some of the swing states, forcing each house to separately consider reasons for objection. During that time, evidence of election irregularities would be presented. They hoped to show election fraud evidence in this nationally covered event, and perhaps convince enough Democrats to vote to refer the contested electors back to their state legislators for reconsideration.

This was certainly no coup attempt. The only ones who would benefit from the violence that occurred were Democrats. The Democrats and media led by Nancy Pelosi, labeling the riots at the Capitol on January 6th as an attempted coup, blamed President Trump for what happened. They then used that misrepresentation to justify a railroaded impeachment of Trump just days before he was due to leave office.

Misrepresenting Trump's speech as a call to violence was quickly expanded by politicians and complicit media to label any discussion of election fraud as inciting violence. This was then expanded to discussions expressing other viewpoints contrary to the complicit narrative. Tens of thousands of individuals have been censored, shadow-banned, or removed from social media, web platforms, YouTube sites, and marketing venues, merely for voicing viewpoints, and citing facts contrary to the Democrat's narrative rhetoric.

APRIL 2021

As I write this in April 2021, the fruits of tyranny are plain to see by all who are not blinded by the communications monopoly. Since the November 2020 election, Democrat factions raced to close down any opposition that might expose their corruption and tyrannical intentions. They concertedly work to silence, discredit, delegitimize, and criminalize anyone voicing opposing opinions. They are acting swiftly to change election laws and the makeup of Congress and the Supreme Court to ensure their ability to control both future election outcomes, and all branches of the federal government.

At the same time, President Biden and the Democrat-controlled Congress pursue swift actions that, contrary to euphemistic titles, cannot help but bring impoverishing burdens upon poor and middle-class Americans, while also making our nation vulnerable to domination by foreign powers. All their actions occur at an overwhelming pace and abundance.

President Biden has already issued over one hundred executive orders, memos, and other actions, and Congress passed a flurry of bills with little debate or consideration that have wide-ranging consequences. The newly inaugurated president proceeds as if he has dictatorial authority. A look at some of these acts reveals the malicious and tyrannical intent of Democrats and the complicit media and corporations.

OUT-OF-CONTROL SPENDING

With the slimmest of margins, Democrats in Congress continue to push for trillions of dollars of additional spending, euphemistically labeled as COVID relief, infrastructure improvements, etc. In reality, the overwhelming portion of this spending goes to benefit Democrat Party interests. It is all deficit spending, using borrowed or newly created money.

Biden's spending proposals are not just one-time expenditures, but include new programs that create annually recurring expenses. They claim they can pay for the increases in spending with more taxes on the "rich." The party that for years claimed it stands for the poor and middle class engages in spending that drives down the real incomes of poorer and middle-class families.

The short-term winners of their spending are China and complicit US corporations, who market large quantities of consumer goods made in China to US customers. The US corporations enabling and profiting from Chinese production also support the Democrat policies while ignoring, covering for, and even benefiting from, atrocities the Communist Party inflicts on their own citizens.

The raiding of capital markets by the Federal government makes reinvigoration of domestic industries displaced by production from Communist China almost impossible. A portion of the excess spending by Congress quickly goes into coffers of the Chinese Communist government, which they use to prepare to destroy and overcome the United States of America.

ENABLING VIOLATION OF IMMIGRATION LAWS

In his first days in office, Biden unilaterally reversed the Trump administration's efforts to enforce US immigration laws and intentionally invited a massive influx of illegal immigrants to our southern border. The primary existence for a federal government is the protection and defense of the security and sovereignty of the nation. The oath the president takes includes an affirmation to "preserve, protect and defend the Constitution of the United States." One of the duties of the president specified in the Constitution states, "he shall take Care that the laws be faithfully executed."

The president does not have the authority to decide not to enforce federal laws, and in particular, laws designed to protect the sovereignty of the nation. Biden has gone beyond simply not enforcing laws by encouraging foreigners to violate federal law by entering the US illegally.

In January, the number of illegal crossings was the highest in a decade. In March, the number of new arrivals apprehended was

172,000, more than any month in the last twenty years. In addition, some officials estimate nearly 1,000 people a day are making it past border security, while border agents are overwhelmed by the processing and caring of tens of thousands of children and families.[62] Those that make it past border agents include criminals taking advantage of the distraction caused by the surge.

Candidate Biden and the media criticized Trump for four years regarding the care of unaccompanied children at the border, but within two months in office, the conditions and numbers of illegal alien children at the border are worse than ever and out of control. Officials for the administration tried to keep journalists and members of Congress from viewing or photographing their facilities. The president hasn't just created a crisis, he is in violation of federal law and his oath of office.

CANCEL KEYSTONE

Keystone is a crude petroleum pipeline. Its purpose is to enable transportation of oil being produced in Alberta, Canada, and North Dakota to US refineries. Such pipelines represent the most cost- and energy-efficient and least-polluting method of transportation of crude oil. The Alberta-based owner of the pipeline committed to making it operate with zero carbon emissions within ten years.[63]

The petroleum being produced in Canada will be shipped for sale somewhere. The most efficient market to supply is the United States. The next most likely customer is Communist China, and shipping to them will require greater carbon emissions for transportation. Some of the Canadian petroleum may still be sent to the US, but will be sent by more energy-consuming, polluting, and costly methods. Biden's justification for the cancelation was global climate crisis.

Canceling the pipeline will not reduce global carbon emissions—it will increase them.

The pipeline is a private enterprise. Construction of the line is done by private firms employing union labor. Federal government involvement consists of approval of a permit to allow pipeline construction and operation. There are those that see the permit approval by the Trump administration as controversial, but there was a process involved including notices, hearings, etc. The permit was not granted until Trump's third year in office. The cancelation of the permit by President Biden was done on his first day in office without any due process. This is how a dictator rules.

The cancelation resulted in the immediate loss of thousands of jobs, significant loss of investment by the Canadian firm paying for the project, and losses by local businesses and governments along the route, who made investments in anticipation of the line. It is a slap in the face to our Canadian allies to the north, including First Nations people, who stood to benefit from the production. It is an unnecessary blow to the economy that has already resulted in increased prices for fuel. It also compromises national security by making us vulnerable to relying on potentially unfriendly sources for our energy needs.

If this decision is allowed to stand, as well as similar ones being made by Biden, we set a precedent giving the president dictatorial authority absent of due process. This type of tyranny led the Founders to declare their independence from England. Furthermore, investors and foreign nations can no longer trust the United States to keep its word and honor our commitments.

ENABLE ELECTION FRAUD LAW

The euphemistic title of Congressional House Bill HR-1, "For the People Act," hides the intent of Democrats. This bill takes control of elections out of the state's purview and places it in the hands of the federal government, and more specifically, in the hands of the party in control of Congress. This runs in direct conflict with the Constitution. Giving all control to one central government puts individual rights and freedoms in jeopardy, because the control over elections throughout the nation then resides in the hands of a few powerful individuals.

The bill includes items that remove safeguards to election fraud. It institutionalizes all the elements listed earlier that Democrats pushed for in 2020 that enables fraud on a large scale. Nearly every developed nation in the world with free elections have basic requirements to qualify those who may vote in national elections: Citizenship, registration prior to the day of election and a form of identification. Most nations do not allow no-excuse mail-in voting. Those that do, have safeguards in place to ensure against fraud. Nearly all nations that have mail-in options have a hard mail-in deadline that coincides with in-person election day voting.

Passage of an HR-1 type bill will not be "for the people," it will be for the entrenched Democrat Party leaders in Congress and the White House. This bill gives them control over the election process. It gives them all the elements they have been seeking for years that enables vote manipulation. It gives them the ability to maintain their positions of power and authority like other tyrants around the world.

PACKING THE COURT

Just twenty-two days before the 2020 general election, Joe Biden stated on WKRC-TV that he is "not a fan of court-packing." This reiterated what he had stated in 1983 in a Senate Judiciary Committee hearing, when he criticized Franklin Roosevelt's attempt to do so in the 1930s. He also expressed disapproval of the idea in 2019 during a Democrat Party debate, yet three months after he was sworn in as president, Biden formed a committee to consider reforming the Supreme Court. Biden took this action despite the hands-off approach the Court took regarding the 2020 election.

Since 1869, there have been nine justices on the Supreme Court. In 1937, President Franklin Roosevelt floated a proposal to Congress to add justices to give him control over the Court. Roosevelt was frustrated by the Supreme Court's previous rejection of several parts of his New Deal legislation. Although Democrats won an overwhelming majority in both houses of Congress and the White House in the 1936 election, packing the Supreme Court met significant resistance from Democrats, as well as Republicans and the public at large, and was never brought to a vote.

Early in our nation's history, politics resulted in manipulations of the structure of the Court, but since 1869, every Congress avoided politicizing the Supreme Court to the extent of modifying their numbers. Today in 2021, the Democrat leadership, with no overwhelming majority, is pushing a controversial agenda destructive to the security of our nation. Their efforts include subverting the separation of powers intended by the Constitution. Proposals to pack the Supreme Court, particularly under these circumstances, show a blatant effort to subjugate the authority of the Court to the desires of the ruling radicals in Congress.

The actions taken by the Democrat Party in the opening months of 2021 defy sound reasoning and appropriate fiscal restraint. Several run counter to the intent and wording of the Constitution, and in some cases, violate existing federal law. For this to be allowed to happen, a majority of members of Congress must be ignorant of the consequences, or complicit with the implications, of these actions. Further a sizeable portion of citizens must be ignorant of the true outcome of the actions being pursued. For this to happen, truth has been displaced by the lies of the rhetoric.

CHAPTER 17

WHEN TRUTH DIES

False words are not only evil in themselves, but they infect the soul with evil."

Plato

"There are, besides, eternal truths, such as Freedom,, etc., that are common to all states of society. But Communism abolishes eternal truths, it abolishes all religion and all morality, instead of constituting them on a new basis; it therefore acts in contradiction to all past historical experience."

Karl Marx, 1848

They all deceive their neighbors, and no one speaks the truth; they have taught their tongues to speak lies; they commit iniquity and are too weary to repent. Oppression upon oppression, deceit upon deceit! They refuse to know me, says the Lord.

Jeremiah 9:5–6 (NRSV)

TRADING TRUTH FOR LIES

For tyranny to prevail and reign, the truth must be perverted and displaced by lies. This is the goal of propaganda. Sway a portion of the population to believe the lie, and they then can be used to sway others or create division. Tyrants find either outcome useful. When lies become accepted as truth in society, the morals, heritage, and fundamentals that united and motivated that people become warped and disregarded. Divisions and chaos cultivated by propaganda destabilize the citizenry and their institutions, enabling the tyrant to prevail.

Stop and think about some things that you are being told you should accept as truth. Are these truths that advance our society, or distortions and lies that create division and undue confusion in our nation?

- *A man can become a woman, and it is fair to allow a biological man to compete in women's sporting events if he decides he should be a woman.* This defies biological facts and Biblical truth. A man can make cosmetic alterations to his body to render the appearance of a woman, but biologically, genetically, he is still a man with male musculoskeletal features and abilities. There are clear physiological differences between men and women that are determined genetically. Surgeries and drugs cannot change a person's genetic makeup. Costume and cosmetic changes do not resolve a person's mental, emotional, and spiritual concerns.
- *A mother's unrestricted, on-demand decision to terminate her near-term baby, that could be viably delivered, is considered abortion.* Discussions of this have gone so far as to suggest that a baby removed alive in a late-term abortion may be allowed

to die from neglect. Only a depraved mind can conceive that this is anything but murder. Unrestricted late-term abortion even defies Roe vs Wade.

- *Censorship is an appropriate response to speech that you disagree with.* Rather than debate issues in open discussions, more and more traditional and social media organizations favoring the liberal Democrat agenda choose to obfuscate facts and opinions contrary to theirs. This directly contradicts the intent and spirit of the Constitution, and enables tyranny to take root and propagate among those that the dominant media favor.

- *Disruption of the traditional nuclear family is an appropriate response to racial disparities, and defending the Biblical and long-standing traditional view of marriage, is racist and homophobic.* Disruption of the nuclear family is a tenet of the founders of Black Lives Matter (BLM). This runs counter to overwhelming evidence that the destruction of the nuclear family, involving a loving father and mother raising their children together in the same home, leads to a host of social problems including higher crime rates, child abuse, lower academic performance, and poverty.[64][65][66][67][68] There is clear evidence that the traditional family structure has suffered to a much greater extent in inner-city black communities than others.[69][70] Denigrating those who seek to uphold the Biblical view of marriage, as a sacred commitment between a man and a woman, runs counter to abundant factual data that demonstrate the assault on the traditional nuclear family has been destructive to society. The narratives that confuse and confound the nuclear family, such as same-sex marriage and variable gender identity, do not represent reasoned compassion, but rather contribute directly to the host of societal problems.

- *The commandments and teachings of the Bible are outdated, and Christians should revise their beliefs to conform to today's understandings.* This is an opinion that is not always stated directly, but is carried out in the actions and words of many inside and outside the western Christian church. Throughout the Bible, people of God faced constant temptation and ridicule presented by worldly forces. Today those forces seem exceptionally strong and concerted. For example, in the last sixty years, the several millennia-old institution of marriage as a sacred union between a man and a woman has been decimated. During the 1960s' attitudes regarding the sacred commitment of marriage began to erode. Most recently, in less than two decades, the multi-millennia tradition of marriage as being between a man and a woman was rendered by various state and federal courts as a violation of individual rights. These decisions confound and confuse the concept of marriage as the union of a man and woman that results in human procreation, and has disrupted the family unit where children are raised by their father and mother. In 2015, the US Supreme Court upheld gay marriage as valid in a 5-4 decision. Chief Justice John Roberts' dissent, presciently warns that this would lead to a direct assault on religious liberties of Christians. As he predicted, efforts have been exerted to force Christian denominations and individuals to conform their beliefs to accept the worldly redefinition of marriage. The court decisions represent a direct violation of the First Amendment, where the government is establishing doctrine that Christians must adhere to.

- *Removing dead people and illegal aliens from voter registration rolls is voter suppression.* This absurd argument has been used in courts to avoid cleaning voter rolls. Federal and state laws call for keeping voter registrations current. The computer database technologies we have today should make such work relatively simple. Failure by county and state officials to remove people who have died, and to prevent ineligible people from registering and voting, is inexcusable.

- *All white people are inherently racist, and our nation was founded to preserve slavery.* Critical Race Theory and the 1619 Project of *NY Times Magazine*, abound with distortions and false narratives to build a case that runs counter to historical facts. A valid theory accurately explains the real world. CRT and the 1619 Project fail to explain the elections of Barack Obama, the popularity of antislavery books in the 1800s, the over 300,000 white Union soldiers who died fighting in opposition to slavery, the Thirteenth Amendment, The Civil Rights Acts of 1964 and 1965, the millions of racially mixed couples in the US, the abundance of prominent and well-to-do blacks including athletes, entertainers, business professionals, entrepreneurs, politicians, Rev. Dr. Martin Luther King Jr., Thurgood Marshall, Clarence Thomas, Patrisse Khan-Cullors, or Nicole Hannah-Jones. Ironically, the apparent acceptance of CRT and 1619 by many white persons, believing they represent a solution to racism is itself contrary to what the proponents of those theories espouse.

This list could go on and on. Note that the one hundred years of Jim Crow laws and overt persecution of blacks from 1865 to 1965 were created, enforced, and perpetuated by Democrats. In 1965, Republicans voted in greater percentages for the Civil Rights Act than Democrats in both the House and Senate. Indeed, despite a sizable

Democrat majority in the House, the Civil Rights Act would not have passed without the strong support of Republicans.

While we are distracted by the flurry of irresponsible executive orders, destructive spending, spurious legislative actions, and false rhetoric, our enemies continue unabated in their pursuit of our demise. The failure of individuals in leadership positions on the national level to prioritize their focus on the threats to our nation's existence is unconscionable.

Rather than focus on actions to ensure the future security of our nation, in the first several months of 2021, Biden and the Democrat leadership in Congress have done just the opposite. The Democrats and their allied media and corporations, in their blind pursuit of power, vilify their political opponents across the aisle as our nation's enemy, while leaving real enemies with free rein to pursue agendas aimed at our downfall. Among those enemies, the greatest threat today, outside our own nation, is Communist China.

CHAPTER 18

THE STEALTH DRAGON

"Communism is not love. Communism is a hammer which we use to crush the enemy."

Mao Zedong, 1950

A PRESENT SEARCH

Before Christmas, 2020, I went shopping online for a pottery wheel as a possible Christmas present. I Googled "best pottery wheels." The first item generated by the search was "buyersguide.org/pottery-wheels/," listing the top ten pottery wheels for 2020. All ten of the items were offered by Chinese companies. Seven of the ten looked exactly alike except for the brand name, color of the units, and minor variations in control switches. Two others appeared to be economy versions that were identical except for labeling, and one was a product designed for children.

Next to each listing is a prominent "Buy at Amazon" button you can click on to immediately purchase the product you chose. I had a hard time believing the top ten wheels were all produced in China, and that seven of the ten could look exactly the same and still be considered different enough to warrant separate listings. I did a little more searching and found a rating of the top five choices of an American art professor. The first four were made in the US by well-established art supply manufacturers. I also checked with a local art supply store, and they also preferred American brands.

This caused me to research the Chinese companies on the "Top 10 List." Most of the ones I could find information on appeared to be shell companies registered in California. They had no website, just business registrations with a Chinese-named registered agent. One with an actual website showed their company location was in China.

I then checked out buyersguide.org. They had top ten lists for just about anything. Not all products were sold by Chinese companies, but every item had a direct link to Amazon. Also, the listings were not chosen by experts, not by humans, but by algorithms. My story illustrates the pervasive influence China and US tech giants exert on the American public, and reveals a relatively innocent aspect of a much greater and more sinister intent on the part of the Chinese government and their American collaborators.

DARK SIDE OF THE CCP

China is governed by the Chinese Communist Party (CCP). The CCP controls every aspect of life of their citizens. If you are in business in China, you will not be allowed to succeed and thrive without abiding by CCP dictates. Any discoveries, information, technologies, and prospects you acquire become accessible to the government, including the People's Liberation Army (PLA, the military of China). The CCP, large Chinese businesses and industrial companies, and the PLA, are essentially one unified conglomerate, operating in concert toward the goal of Chinese world supremacy.

The leader in China, Xi Jinping, is the General Secretary of the CCP, Chairman of the Central Military Commission, and has been president of the Peoples' Republic of China since 2013. He ended presidential term limits in 2018, and through a so-called anti-corruption campaign that he imposed, has removed and discredited many potential rivals to secure his totalitarian rule.

China acquires technology from around the world in every way it can, legitimately, or otherwise. Their welcome to companies and academics from other nations gives them access to the latest technologies, including ones directly applicable to their military. They have companies and individuals distributed throughout the world, constantly seeking to develop academic, business, and government contacts and relationships.

They leverage their contacts to develop, glean, or steal information. This information includes scientific, technological, medical, financial, governmental, military, and biometric data. It includes the personal medical and financial information of millions of Americans.

Their agents worldwide also promote and enforce the official narratives of CCP propaganda. In the United States, they influence the decisions of politicians, corporations, NGOs, media organizations, and even sports leagues. They also strongly influence the narratives many Americans view in news media. In June 2021, the number one news' app in the US, NewsBreak, with forty-five million active users, is owned and operated by CCP connected operatives.[71]

They initiate and support schools, seminars, and collaborative research centers that create dual opportunities to disseminate rhetoric favorable to their goals while gathering more information and innovations from unsuspecting Americans. They channel funding to nonprofit and political organizations that help promote their domination agenda. In some cases, well-intentioned American recipients of support become unwitting accomplices of the CCP.

Chinese initiatives seek and offer business ventures in other nations. This is particularly enticing to underdeveloped and developing nations. Once established, the nation becomes obliged to the CCP and either complies with increased concessions or suffer the consequences of losing their support. Chinese communications giant Huawei is presently promoting its 5G network to developing nations worldwide, which will give them great influence over what is communicated, as well as a great potential to eavesdrop.

China now has the largest navy in the world and continues to build additional state-of-the-art vessels. The PLA has fifty percent more active members than the United States military. They likely have the largest cyber warfare force. They aggressively pursue technology upgrades to their military systems including cyber, missile, and space capabilities. With Biden assuming the presidency in 2021, China accelerated hostile activities toward Taiwan, Hong Kong, the South China Sea, and India.

For more than twenty years, the CCP has gradually escalated persecution of minority ethnic and religious groups, including Uyghur Muslims, Falun Gong, and Christians. Churches and mosques have been destroyed. In some provinces, having religious symbols, relics, or writings in your own home are a crime. Even Uyghur graveyards have been desecrated and eradicated.

Millions are held in concentration camps, and evidence has shown forced Chinese labor manufacturing products for dozens of companies such as Nike, Adidas, Skechers, Google, Samsung, Amazon, Tesla, Dell, Lenovo, Cisco, HP, and Apple. A bill, the Uyghur Forced Labor Prevention Act, was introduced in Congress in 2020, and again in 2021, to stop manufacturing using forced labor in China to produce items sold by US companies. Companies including Coca-Cola, Costco, Apple, Patagonia, and Nike lobbied to weaken the legislation.

The United States and other western nations have recognized China's treatment of the Uyghur people as genocide. According to Salih

Hudayar, Prime Minister in Exile of Turkestan, hundreds of thousands of Uyghur women have been subjected to forced abortions and mass sterilizations. 850,000 children have been separated from their families and sent to indoctrination camps. Women are raped, and sent away and forced into marriages to Chinese men.

In recent years, reports by agencies in several nations, including the US, UK, and Canada, indicate that Uyghur Muslims have been the victims of organ harvesting. Tens of thousands of healthy Uyghurs are reportedly killed each year to provide organs to recipients who travel to China from around the world. Reports include harvesting organs while the victim is still alive, and in a few reports, without anesthesia. Ominously, Chinese authorities have collected genetic and biometric information from an estimated twelve million Uyghurs.

DEALING WITH THE DEVIL

Do a search for quotes by Xi Jinping, and the first sites in the search provide quotes that give you the impression he is a benevolent, peace-loving leader who seeks equitable dealings with the US and other nations. Consider this frequently cited quote by him:

"During the long process of history, by relying on our own diligence, courage and wisdom, Chinese people have opened up a good and beautiful home where all ethnic groups live in harmony and fostered an excellent culture that never fades."

How does this square with the previous paragraphs? The positive face the CCP works tirelessly to portray to the world dissolves, when the curtain is pulled back, to reveal the reality of their actions and intentions.

Reality is even more disconcerting when we recognize that apologists for the CCP abound in our own nation. Politicians, dominant tech and media, corporations and individuals with lucrative Chinese connections, colleges and universities, and even professional sports organizations, toe the line for their Chinese benefactors. Why are we not extricating ourselves from the economic entanglements we have created with them? How can we justify continuing to enrich them, and provide them with our technology, thereby enabling them to overtake us?

This is not new news. Why is there not widespread outrage about this? Why has the 2021 Congress and the president been focused on doing things that damage our economy while ignoring the Chinese threat? Given the obvious lack of manufacturing capabilities of the US exposed by the COVID crisis, why was there no priority placed on restoring American production abilities? Why was this not first on the list, instead of encouraging illegal border crossings, closing beneficial pipeline construction, bankrupting the US Treasury with irresponsible wasteful spending, and pushing for centralized control over national elections that would give the dominant party in power control comparable to the CCP in China?

How can we morally justify our relationships with China? Tens of millions of Chinese citizens have died at the hands of the CCP under Mao and his successors. Today Mao is revered in China by the CCP like a patron saint. The CCP continues committing atrocities as heinous as those perpetrated by Hitler's Nazi Germany, and the trend is toward greater oppression.

Frequently I saw and heard Democrats and their surrogates comparing Republicans to Nazi fascists. Such comparisons were never valid, and they diminish the atrocities committed under Hitler. Today, the Nazi holocaust comparison to China is valid. Will we take this seriously?

While making that comparison, it is frightening to see parallels to the Nazi era and what transpired in the last year in our own nation. It brings me to question the true intentions and loyalties of the current leadership in our nation's Capital. I have great misgivings and fear that those presently wielding power in Washington, DC, not only lack the capacity to appropriately respond to the threat we face in China, but surreptitiously support the CCP agenda. Empty lip service, and compliant corporations, do nothing to allay my fears.

THE WRONG CONCLUSIONS

Communism requires that people be judged by their social status. Anyone who materially excels that does not conform to the party line is deemed unworthy and stripped of their wealth. The traditional ruling and wealthy classes are removed from power by those promising changes for the better for the working classes. Those enforcing the changes become the authorities in power. The only way those who are in authority can maintain their positions is to co-opt or eliminate other potential competitors and convince the citizenry to believe their place in life is to serve the common good by conforming to the dictates of the new authorities. It creates what it claims to oppose, a ruling class. In China, the ruling class is the CCP.

Reverend Dr. Martin Luther King Jr dreamed that his children would not be judged by their color. Critical Race Theory (CRT) requires that people should be judged by their color. Fundamentally, CRT claims that judging people by their color will eliminate racism. This begins with a conflicting premise, and only serves to accentuate discrepancies. Just as Marxism teaches to judge others by their class, CRT teaches we should judge others by their color. Those who propose CRT and other Marxist solutions may perceive a valid problem, but then draw the wrong conclusions.

Coming to the wrong conclusion, leads to proposing solutions that fail to solve the perceived problem. When presented with a problem, the natural reaction is something needs to be fixed, something needs to change. A problem is perceived, and then someone comes along stating they can change things for the better.

For many people that is enough, and they go along with the one who promises a change for the better. Karl Marx sought to change the world with his dream of communism, "The philosophers have only interpreted the world in various ways; the point is to change it."[72] The change promises great things to come, but when you pull back the curtain, you see the suffering and tragedies that will result from the change they have in mind.

What was Barack Obama's slogan when he first ran for president? "Change we can believe in." It was expressed in different phrases, but they all focused on the word "change." I know several people who voted for him simply because they felt it was time for a change. Today in mid-2021, the Biden administration is populated with radical social-ist carryovers from the Obama administration. Some have decidedly communist ideologies, and are pushing to foist them upon the nation, particularly our children. It is critical that Americans recognize their rhetoric for what it is, and that their policies are based upon faulty conclusions. Central to the false rhetoric are claims about racial dispar-ities in our nation.

CHAPTER 19

BLACK LIVES

"Wise statesmen as they were, they knew the tendency of prosperity to breed tyrants, and so they established these great self-evident truths, that when in the distant future some man, some faction, some interest, should set up the doctrine that none but rich men, or none but white men, were entitled to life, liberty and the pursuit of happiness, their posterity might look up again to the Declaration of Independence and take courage to renew the battle which their fathers began – so that truth, and justice, and mercy, and all the humane and Christian virtues might not be extinguished from the land; so that no man would hereafter dare to limit and circumscribe the great principles on which the temple of liberty was being built."

Abraham Lincoln, August 17, 1858, conclusion of his speech
in Lewiston, Illinois, on the Declaration of Independence.

JULY 2020

On May 25, 2020, an unarmed black man in handcuffs named George Floyd died while being restrained by police officers in Minneapolis. The response to the death was rapid and dramatic. Protests both peaceful and violent broke out not only in Minneapolis, but in cities in various parts of the nation. Two sides quickly formed up, one sympathizing with the protesters complaining of racial bias by police, and another side decrying the riot violence and looting, and pointing out the isolated nature of the incident compared with the 300 million or so police encounters with the public each year.

In our nation today racial tension and animosity clearly exists. The political division of the nation does nothing to alleviate or rectify our racial issues. Instead, like the other disconnected issues I point to in this book, political division serves to isolate each side and prevent rational discourse and meaningful pathways to solutions.

MINNEAPOLIS

One thing that everyone agrees on about George Floyd's death is that it was tragic. So why did two sides develop so quickly? A look at Minneapolis itself is illuminating.

Minneapolis is one of the most segregated cities in the nation. A paper published by the Institute of Metropolitan Opportunity in 2015 sought the reason for that.[73] The paper suggests segregation resulted in part due to policies that promoted equal opportunity housing in existing low-income areas concentrating minorities in those select areas. One statistic from the paper states that in eighty-three schools in the Minneapolis area, nonwhites comprise more than 90% of the student body. This in a state that is 84% white.[74]

Higher-crime areas of Minneapolis correspond closely with the low-income minority concentrated areas. The intersection of Chicago Ave and E 38th St. where George Floyd was killed, lies along a corridor of segregation parallel to Interstate 35. In an op-ed article, previous Minneapolis Mayor Betsy Hodges states that police activity is concentrated in higher-crime segregated neighborhoods. Hodges, a member of the Democratic-Farmer-Labor Party, blames the disproportionate activity on liberal white elites who block reformation efforts.

TRAGIC FACTS

Tragically, murder is too common in segregated black inner-city neighborhoods. Looking at CDC overall cause of death statistics for the United States, death by homicide is not close to the top fifteen causes. The tragedy becomes visible when you look at causes of death by age range. For the age range of fifteen to twenty-nine, for all races combined, death by homicide ranks as the third leading cause of death behind unintended accidents and suicide. For black men from the age of fifteen thru thirty-four, homicide is the leading cause of death, and for black boys ages one to fourteen it is the second leading cause of death. In 2017, CDC data indicates for ages ten to forty-nine, black males account for half of all homicide victims.[75]

To provide a visual perspective of this problem, I prepared the chart in Figure 3. This chart shows the percentage of deaths by homicide by age. This graphic dramatically shows that all black males from age one to sixty are more likely to die from homicide than their white male counterparts, and black males in their teens and twenties are ten times more likely to die by homicide than white males.

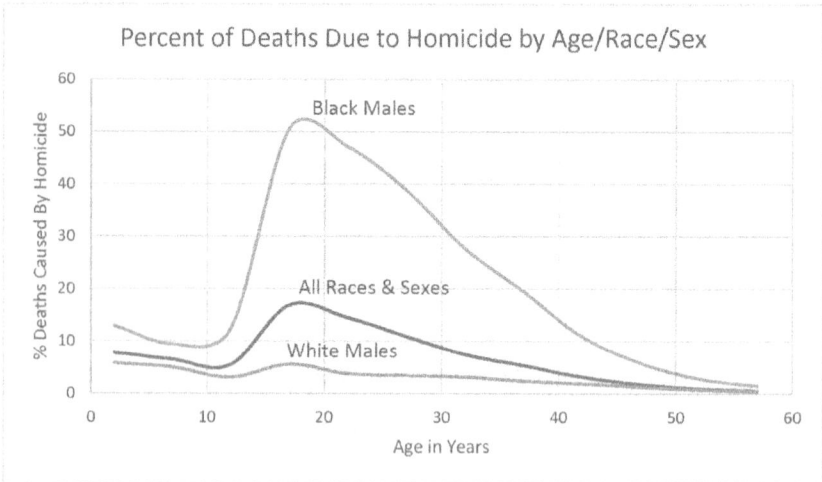

Figure 3. Percent of deaths due to homicide by age in the United States in 2017 for all races and sexes combined, non-Hispanic white males only, and non-Hispanic black males only.[76]

The graph in Figure 3 does not account for the fact that not all blacks are in the same socioeconomic status. Homicide deaths are much more likely to occur in poorer segregated neighborhoods. The odds of dying by homicide for a young black man in a poor, segregated inner-city neighborhood may be in the range of eighteen times greater than for a young white male.

It is important to note this is not a black against white problem. FBI statistics that compile homicides where the race of both the victim and the offender are known for the year 2018 show that 81% of white victims were killed by white offenders, and 89% of black victims were killed by black offenders.[77] We are segregated even in how we murder each other.

Of the many black men I have known in my time, I have not observed any greater propensity toward violence than I have in men of other races. The tendency toward violence I see in others depends upon how they were raised and with whom they associate. So where does this anomaly of black male homicide come from?

FAMILIES LOST

An overwhelming abundance of studies and literature show that single-parent households, and particularly fatherless families, correspond to a variety of negative outcomes for children, including violent crime.[78][79] This correlation has been known for decades and is observed not just in the United States but throughout the world.[80] A state-by-state analysis in the US found that a ten percent increase in children living in single-parent homes accompanies a seventeen percent increase in juvenile crime.[81] This correlation does not imply that all single-parent homes result in delinquent children, but two surveys of incarcerated youths in 1987 and 1994 found that 70% to 87% respectively of juveniles in custody came from single-parent families.[82]

Although the absence of fathers affects all children in varying degrees, there exists a wide gap between blacks and other races in the number of unmarried single mothers raising children. In 2014, the percentages of children living with both of their married biological parents were 70% for non-Hispanic whites, 59% for Hispanic whites, and 33% for black children.[83] A Pew Research study also done in 2014, found that 71% of births to black women occurred outside of marriage while unmarried women accounted for only 29% of white births.[84] The data clearly show that children need fathers, and more than half of all black children grow up without fathers.

In the early to mid-20th century, marriage rates between black and white women were similar.[85] Divorce rates for both white and black women began to increase preceding the decline in marriage from 1940 to 1980. However, the divorce increase and marriage decline occurred faster in black populations. By 2012, nearly 90% of white women had married by the age of forty-four compared to 62% of black women of the same age. In the same year, 73% of white women married by age forty-four remained married and lived with their spouse, compared with only 53% of black women of the same age who had ever married. This means by age forty-four only 33% of black women compared to 65% of white women were married and living with their husband.

The preceding shows a striking correlation between the breakdown of traditional marriage and the rise of crime and other social ills. The decline of marriage and its associated negative consequences has hit black populations faster and harder than others. This represents a national tragedy. If our nation is to be redeemed, the marriage decline must be reversed.

THE GREAT FALL

Many reasons are put forth to explain the precipitous decline of marriage in black communities. Humans are fundamentally all similar. The faults, joys, motivations, desires, sins, and emotions I read of people 4,000 to 2,000 years ago in the Bible, are the same I see in myself and others today. Understanding the causes requires the conclusion there is no difference in motivations between black and white. As Mandisa sings in her song, "we all bleed the same."[86]

Given this, an objective view of statistics shows a bimodal effect on our society since the end of World War II. To explain the downward trend of all races, together with the more drastic decline of marriage in blacks, at least two causes are required, one affecting all of society and one specific to the black community.

One society-wide cause pointed to by many, involves the unintended consequences of government programs such as the war on poverty launched in the mid-1960s. Government policies may influence and contribute to the decline in marriage rates in lower-income families, but I see a larger and more devastating cause in the US.

The nationwide decline in marriage reflects the gradual sea-change in the morals and values of our society. The sexual revolution of the 1960s to 1980s, and parallel women's liberation movement, played into the accepting minds of the self-centered Baby Boomer population.

The tumultuous 1960s opened the door for popularized phrases such as, "Do your own thing," and "Love the one you're with." Apparel styles became more sensuous. Movie and television censorship standards were relaxed or ignored. In 1969, most significantly to our topic, California changed divorce laws to allow for no-fault divorces. All other states quickly followed California's example.

In two decades, we went from a society that valued marriage as a sacred commitment of fidelity for a lifetime, to an optional contract where if one spouse felt unfulfilled or dissatisfied for any reason, they could easily end the relationship. From 1960 to 1980 the divorce rate more than doubled—the compounding rate of divorces year after year magnified the negative effect on children. In 1950, only 11% of children saw their parent's part due to divorce, whereas 50% of children born to married couples in the 1970s experienced their parent's divorce.[87]

The deep social changes experienced by the United States in the last sixty years represents a shift from a society guided by a higher moral authority to one where individuals determine their own set of rights, values, and morals. We have historical precedent for societies that follow this trend. A central underlying theme of the entire Old Testament of the Bible illustrates the result when society rejects the moral higher authority for their own self-interests. The result always ends in tragedy and suffering.

THE REALITY OF RACISM

We infer by the two-to-one ratio between black and white marriage rates that the societal moral decline, and possibly governmental policies with unintended consequences, accounts for only half of the drop in black marriages. This indicates the presence of a unique aspect of the black population that separates them from others. The obvious aspect to consider is a racial bias.

Racial bias against blacks in America began early during European colonization. Justification of enslavement of black Africans in America by white Europeans resulted in popularization of the absurd concept that blacks are an inferior race. This led to various laws in the past restricting life for black individuals.

After the Civil War, despite the end of slavery, laws were passed by local governments and states that restricted where blacks could go and what they could do. This began in former Confederate states, but as blacks migrated throughout the country, laws limiting black opportunities spread throughout the nation.

A Supreme court ruling in 1896 legalized separate facilities for blacks, as long as they were equal, and resulted in laws restricting access by blacks to white-only public waiting rooms, restrooms, swimming pools, phone booths, hospitals, drinking fountains, schools, parks, theaters, restaurants, and jails.[88] In the South, enforcement of restrictions included violence and murder by organizations such as the Ku Klux Klan. Many cities restricted where blacks could live. In Minneapolis, real estate deeds included restrictive covenants that limited where blacks could buy homes.[89] Those past restrictions are why Minneapolis is so segregated today.

Jim Crow-type laws remained in force until Congress passed the Civil Rights Act of 1964. Three years later, the Fair Housing Act addressed discrimination in housing. Despite landmark laws, statistics show bias persists. For example, data for the last sixteen years reveal that blacks are twice as likely as whites to be turned down on a loan application for a new home.[90] Whether intentionally, or subconsciously, the net effect is the same. Although laws officially ended segregation, our society still struggles to achieve real integration in portions of our society.

THE PROGENY OF RACISM

To understand the marriage gap between blacks and whites, we need to look at other racial gaps. The first is unemployment. Bureau of Labor Statistics data from 1950 to the present show a consistent black unemployment rate twice that of whites. This gap holds true regardless of the state of the economy. At the beginning of the twentieth century, the unemployment rates between blacks and whites were nearly equal. At that time over 50% of blacks worked in agriculture, mostly on southern cotton farms.

In the 1910s and 1920s blacks began migrating in significant numbers north for higher-paying manufacturing jobs. As more blacks moved to northern cities, the communities they relocated to became less welcoming, resulting in residential and school segregation. Furthermore, they were generally consigned to less desirable lower-paying laborer positions and more likely to be laid off first before their white counterparts.[91] [92]

In the 1930s and 1940s, blacks suffered high unemployment rates along with everyone else, but the tendency to be preferentially laid off first led to a rising gap between blacks and their white coworkers. Further, some programs designed to aid lower-income families failed to benefit blacks as much as whites. For example, FHA loans to lower-income individuals could not be used to buy in black or mixed neighborhoods.[93] Thus, migration for better pay resulted in less stable employment and substandard living accommodations.

The incarceration rate is the second important gap. Incarceration rates of blacks into federal prisons were near the same proportion as the US population at large until the mid-1930s. State prison admission rates for blacks were nearly twice that of the general population in the 1920s and early 1930s, and then they began to rise even more. By 1960 combined state and federal rates were three times the total population, and by 1986, the percent of blacks being sent to prison were nearly four times the proportion of blacks in the total US population.[94] In the year 2000, blacks were at least seven times more likely to be in prison compared to their white counterparts. Since that time, the gap has narrowed some, but the proportional number of black men in prison in 2017 was still nearly six times greater than whites.[95]

Census data show a gap between black and white women who were married and living with their spouse at ages forty to forty-five as early as 1930.[96] Although marriage rates of black and white women at that time are comparable, separation and divorce rates accelerated among black couples. The destabilizing effects of segregation, employment limited to unstable low paying jobs with little encouragement for advancement, and discrimination emerging seemingly wherever they moved, began to take a toll on urbanized black families. We see this first in the dissolution of families through divorce, followed by increasing incarceration rates of blacks.

The seeds of discrimination cast across our nation in the twentieth century, gathered from harvests of racism cultivated in the South centuries prior, took root and spread like weeds. We see the breakdown of family units and the first signs of their detrimental effects corresponding with the urban migration of blacks. Ironically, they experienced racial discrimination in the very places they sought to improve their lives and escape racial bias.

In the decades that followed, government policies designed to eliminate societal problems inadvertently exacerbated the decline of marriage among poor black communities. In 1964 we declared war on poverty, disincentivizing young women on welfare from getting married. In 1965 we declared war on crime, resulting in increased arrest rates in poorer communities; the same segregated communities created by racial policies put in place at the beginning of the twentieth century.

In 1971 we declared war on drugs, which intensified the effect of the war on crime. Every administration since then has continued the prosecution of this war. The drug war strategy of mandatory sentences swelled our prison populations.

As these strategies intensified in the 1980s and 1990s, we see a perfect storm of past segregation, and governmental policies, that work particularly against black men. High incarceration rates, higher unemployment, lower average income potential, destabilized lives that inhibit the accumulation of wealth, all combine to make a larger proportion of black men unavailable, or unsuitable, prospects for marriage.[97]

At the same time, an assault by factions within our society that began in the 1950s and 1960s, intensifies against the moral and religious traditions including marriage. This sets up a downward spiral where a greater proportion of children are raised in fatherless homes, resulting in increased crime, lower education levels, and reduced ability to succeed in the working world. This leads to further decline in marital success and continues the downward spiral.

CHAPTER 20

BLM—THE WRONG RESPONSE

"I have a dream that my four little children will one day live in a nation where they will not be judged by the color of their skin but by the content of their character."

Martin Luther King, Jr, speech from the steps of the
Lincoln Memorial on August 28, 1963, during the
March on Washington for Jobs and Freedom

"There is no longer Jew or Greek, there is no longer slave or free, there is no longer male and female, for all of you are one in Christ Jesus."

The Apostle Paul, Letter of Paul to the Galatians, 3:28 (NRSV)

"Our Constitution was made only for a moral and religious people. It is wholly inadequate to the government of any other."

John Adams, 1798

BLACK LIVES MATTER

Black Lives Matter (BLM) represents a passionate response to the racial disparities I have described. BLM and other movements such as CRT and the *New York Times* 1619 project, draw attention to these racial issues. However, they fail to examine the fundamentals of the disparities, and thus draw conclusions that are themselves racially biased, and propose solutions that will not promote prosperity, integration, peace, and unity but will result in just the opposite.

BLM started on July 13, 2013, as a #BlackLivesMatter post in response to the acquittal of George Zimmerman for the shooting death of Trayvon Martin. Three black professional radical women activists, Alicia Garza, Opal Tometi, and Patrisse Khan-Cullors, collaborated to build a movement of protests focused on police violence used against blacks. The movement gained notoriety in 2014 on their Freedom Ride to Ferguson in response to the death of Mike Brown, and recently in the aftermath of the death of George Floyd.[98]

The website blacklivesmatter.com states BLM stands for freedom and justice, liberation, and peace for blacks as well as all people. They acknowledge, respect, and celebrate differences and commonalities. The founders seek to build and nurture loving community and practice empathy. These statements are agreeable, but their flowery language masks a darker side promoting policies that run contrary to freedoms and opportunities that lead to prosperity.

The greatest concern found on their website is in a statement in which they claim to disrupt the nuclear family structure.[99] Their discussion of families conspicuously avoids the use of the word father. There are other statements about family and mothers that also avoid the mention of fathers. We have seen that children raised in fatherless homes are subject to an array of negative outcomes. Restoring the sanctity of the marriage commitment between mother and father is fundamental to nurturing children. The intentional disruption of this vital element will doom any attempts to raise freedoms and living standards in low-income segregated black communities.

Other concerns with BLM involve what the website does not state. The first concern is their Marxist affiliation.[100] History in the last century shows that successful Marxist activism always led to dictatorship and tyranny with little to no improvement in living standards for the masses. In the last one hundred years, over one hundred million citizens lost their lives at the hands of communist dictators ruling with absolute power seized in the aftermath of destruction of social institutions by Marxist activism. This is not the answer that will lift black lives out of poverty and create a truly integrated American society.

My second concern extends from the first. Black Lives Matter collaborated and endorsed the policies enumerated on the website Movement for Black Lives.[101] The policies comprise a wide-ranging list of demands endorsed by BLM.[102] The demands are organized into six generalized categories: End the War on Black People, Reparations, Divest-Invest, Economic Justice, Community Control, and Political Power.

Within the lists are a few items that have some validity. Unfortunately, most of the list suffers from a misunderstanding of how jobs and wealth are created and maintained. They call for outright implementation of Marxist ideals that will destroy the foundations of a free-market economy and representative republic that are the framework that enables prosperity.

Why do liberal politicians, activists, professors, and the dominant corporate media think the formula to raise black citizens from poverty to prosperity should be the opposite from the method that produced prosperity for the rest of Americans? The great material wealth of Americans, including many people of color, results from the practice of free-market economics. Why now raise the cry in the name of black lives to abandon the source of prosperity in exchange for Marxist ideologies and their spawn such as BLM, CRT, and 1619? Why should poor, segregated black populations be denied opportunities that more prosperous populations presently enjoy?

This great irony uncovers a racism of a most insidious kind. The kind that promotes personal and political agendas at the expense of a particular group identified by the color of their skin. A racism that masks indifference behind rhetoric that speaks of great caring efforts while pursuing actions that run counter to the best interests of the people.

All Americans concerned about the division we see in our nation today need to recognize the difference between the empathy for the welfare of black citizens embodied in the expression "black lives matter," and the organization Black Lives Matter. BLM seeks disruption of the foundations of our society, rather than honest solutions for lifting the standard of living and quality of life for Americans in segregated inner-city neighborhoods.

POLITICAL PARTY AFFILIATION

For organizations like BLM, radical activism has become a profession. Protest is an end unto itself. Success is not measured in gains in incomes, greater educational achievement, or reduction in violent crime. Radical activists measure success in the amount of disruption created, how many individuals show up for protests, and how many activists have been trained.

The protest business has become quite lucrative. A 2020 estimate showed that BLM-related groups took in 133 million dollars in donations since 2013.[103] Click the donate button on Black Lives Matter, Movement for Black Lives or other related sites, and you will be taken to the ActBlue website.

ActBlue is a site run by the Democrat Party. Through it, thousands of organizations receive donations, including many Democrat Party candidates, as well as an abundance of progressive organizations.[104] As of mid-August 2020, the site had collected nearly six billion dollars since it began operation in 2004. The description on the ActBlue website states, "Our platform is available to Democratic candidates and committees, progressive organizations, and nonprofits that share our values for no cost besides a 3.95% processing fee on donations."

The ActBlue statement reveals two interesting points. First, the Democrat Party appears to have made over five million dollars on the Black Lives Matter organizations. Second, the Democrat Party implies by this statement that they share the values of Black Lives Matter organizations dominated by Marxist dogma, and positions that denigrate law enforcement officers and traditional nuclear families.

It is not clear from this website where the money goes that you donate. BLM is considered a charity, so the money is funneled through the 501C3 tax-exempt ActBlue entity, AB Charities. This creates a very gray area considering BLM organization's affiliation with the Democrat Party by use of the site, and that BLM organizations supported Hillary Clinton in the 2016 election, and opposed Donald Trump in 2016 and 2020.

This brings me to ask the question, who are you protesting against when you march in a BLM event? Going back to Minneapolis, Minnesota is one of the most Democrat-supporting states in the union. The state voted for the Democrat Party candidate for US president in every election in the last forty years, and only favored two Republican presidential candidates in the last eighty-four years.[105] For the last forty-two years Minneapolis elected a Democrat for mayor, and no Republican won an election for mayor in that city since 1957.[106]

In the last eighty years blacks nationally have overwhelmingly voted for the Democrat presidential candidate.[107] From 1936 to 1960, the black vote varied between 61% and 77% in favor of the Democrat candidate. In 1964, 94% of blacks supported the Democratic nominee. In the presidential campaign of that year, the Democrat Lyndon Johnson supported passage of the Civil Rights Act, while the Republican candidate Barry Goldwater opposed the Act. Since then, unwavering black support for the Democrat presidential candidate ranged from 82% to 95%. The 95% occurred in 2008 to elect Barack Obama president.

In the 1930s, blacks supported Roosevelt based upon severe economic conditions and the promise of actions taken by his administration to alleviate the financial distress. Unfortunately, activities of the government served to destabilize the business environment resulting in waves of layoffs that hit the black population worse than others. Democrats dominated the White House and both houses of Congress from the early 1930s until 1947, while the gap in unemployment between whites and blacks widened, and Jim Crow laws continued to oppress blacks. It was the Democratic Party, particularly in the South, that continued to promote, propagate, and enforce Jim Crow laws.

Today, most of the racial protests around the nation are in segregated cities dominated by Democrat politicians. The political policies and agendas proposed and funded serve the continuation of the status quo, disabling the empowerment of individuals to raise themselves up academically, economically, and socially. They feed the attitude of victim rather than enabling self-reliance and self-confidence to pursue dreams and goals that lead to prosperity and well-being. This has been the case for decades.

The last policy topic in the Movement for Black Lives pamphlet referenced earlier demands Political Power. The black community possesses considerable political power, but every election cycle for the last eighty-eight years, they abdicate that power to the same party. Black voters consistently support Democrat candidates based on political rhetoric, regardless of actual outcomes. Indeed, in our current political climate in 2020–21, the party is charging headlong in the opposite direction away from prosperity. It is the same direction demanded by BLM organizations. Regardless of the rhetoric of some BLM organizers, BLM organizations are simply an extension of the Democrat Party.

I am not a member of any political party because they focus narrowly on their party positions while discounting others. Political parties overlook or defend their own defects, while highlighting faults of their opponents. They place the interests of their party ahead of society at large. These tendencies create conflict and division that impedes the pursuit of beneficial courses of action. Although I find fault in all parties, in the year 2021, I am compelled to specifically denounce the present direction of the Democrat Party.

Rather than celebrate the goodness of the vast majority of Americans rich and poor, black and white, they pursue vindictive persecution of their political opponents. Contrary to the promises of their rhetoric, the radical direction of the Democrat Party, and related organizations such as BLM, promote destructive and divisive agendas. Of even greater concern, they pave the path they travel with moral bankruptcy.

THE CONTENT OF THEIR CHARACTER

In his famous speech from the steps of the Lincoln Memorial on August 28, 1963, during the March on Washington for Jobs and Freedom, Rev. Dr. Martin Luther King Jr. spoke of his dream of racial equality and integration. Part of that dream includes the famous statement, "I have a dream that my four little children will one day live in a nation where they will not be judged by the color of their skin, but by the content of their character." Coming from Rev. Dr. King, that one sentence has powerful and deep meaning.

To desire to be judged by the content of your character, you assume a responsibility upon yourself. As a Christian, that content of character includes the ethics and morality one finds within the pages of the Bible. To seek righteousness in the eyes of God. To practice honesty and truthfulness in all dealings. To acknowledge our human frailties and tendencies, and recognize our need for a savior when confronted by our sinful nature. To love all humanity including those counted as our enemies, even in the face of persecution.

Rev. Dr. Martin Luther King Jr. taught nonviolence as the only appropriate response of a Christian to violence, hatred, and persecution, including the oppression of black Americans. The individuals gathered in Washington DC for the March on August 28, 1963, numbered an estimated 250,000. The march was carefully planned and organized to prevent violence. The organizers, including Rev King, were welcomed to meet with members of Congress, and within three months, what would become the Civil Rights act of 1964, was introduced in the House Rules Committee.

Martin Luther King Jr. promoted civil disobedience as a means of protest, but only in nonviolent and nondestructive ways. Further, the first major action led by him was the Montgomery bus boycott of 1955–1956. That was not civil disobedience—it was a boycott that required considerable inconvenience on the part of the participants. Instead of taking the bus, thousands of blacks carpooled, took a taxi, or walked to and from work and the store. The protest took 381 days, but ultimately succeeded not only in eliminating discrimination in public transportation, but also in bringing national attention to the injustices of discrimination. In doing so, they maintained a considerable moral high ground.

Rev. Dr. King gave a speech at Mason Temple in Memphis the night before his death. At the end of his talk, he prophetically spoke of having been to the mountaintop and seeing the Promised Land. He suggested he may not be able to join his listeners into that land, but that he was not worried and feared no man, proclaiming, "Mine eyes have seen the glory of the coming of the Lord." Just as Jesus, on the night before his crucifixion, spoke to his disciples in the Upper room trying to convey his impending sacrifice, Martin Luther King Jr. alludes to a foreknowledge of events that would transpire the next day.

Perhaps more prophetically, earlier in his speech, he shared a portion of one of his sermons he had given in the wake of the Bus Boycott years earlier that he included in his book Strength to Love.[108] The sermon titled *On Being a Good Neighbor* draws from Jesus' parable of the Good Samaritan, a parable that answers the question, "Who is my neighbor?"[109] In that sermon, he shares the key to ending the racial disparities that continue even to this day in 2021.

The Good Samaritan, traveling the route between Jerusalem and Jericho, found a Jewish man lying along the road naked, bloodied, and dying. Two separate prominent Jewish men had passed by the beaten man, hours before for reasons unstated, but given the isolated nature of the roadway, they may have been afraid for their own lives, and quickly moved on without stopping to lend aid. Although Jewish people of that time treated Samaritans as enemies, the Samaritan stopped, bound up the man's wounds, placed him on his animal, and took him to an inn. There he continued to nurse the injured man.

The next day the Samaritan paid the innkeeper to care for him with the promise that he would pay any additional expenses incurred when the Samaritan returned. Reverend King points out that the Samaritan possessed an altruism that was at once universal, dangerous, and excessive. The man had compassion unlimited by nationality or race, disregarded the potential danger to himself, and willingly went far beyond the call of duty.

Martin Luther King Jr. introduces observations made by Dr. Harry Emerson Fosdick regarding enforceable and unenforceable obligations. Written laws of governments represent enforceable obligations, while unenforceable obligations compel us by personal convictions we possess in our hearts. The two prominent Jewish men committed no crime passing by the beaten man. The Samaritan man responded in a way that no law compelled him to. The Samaritan responded to an unenforceable obligation. Reverend King points to this parable to show that passing laws cannot change what is in a person's heart. Eliminating prejudice and bringing real integration only comes when people submit their hearts to unenforceable obligations.

It is in the spiritual heart of humans where the great virtues and ills of society rise and fall. Attempts to solve societal disparities by government policies devoid of attention to the human soul will fail. The content of a person's character includes our willingness to oblige ourselves to obey the call to love our neighbors. Jesus' definition of our neighbor includes those we call enemy, and even those who despise us and call us enemy.

REALIZING THE DREAM

In 1967 Martin Luther King Jr was extremely critical of the federal government for the inadequate implementation of the "War on Poverty." He called it piecemeal, misguided, and underfunded. I admire Dr. King both as a Christian and as a civil rights leader. He became a driving force behind the strides to eliminate discrimination in public facilities, businesses, voting, and schools. He maintained a high moral ground in the fight for equal rights.

The shift from the enforcement of rights to the demand for funding from the federal government marked a shift that would lead to disappointment. The war on poverty assumes that government possesses the solution to the attitudes that often result in impoverished circumstances. To Rev. Dr. Martin Luther King Jr's dismay, he saw the federal government could not be relied upon for an economic solution.

Poverty is as much or more a societal and spiritual issue, as it is an economic one. Simply writing and handing out checks will not bring about changes in perspective, attitude, ethics, and financial acumen that enables people socialized in poverty to elevate their incomes, equity, and quality of life. Poverty does not discriminate, but the past extreme oppression and segregation of many black citizens in the US, place them as a group in a clear disadvantaged state. The societal ills that plague impoverished black communities are symptoms of the combination of racially induced poverty and the moral decline of our society. To find a solution, we need to look not at government, but at ourselves.

Impoverished communities do not need more programs spawned from divisive government, resulting in continued poverty and strife. Martin Luther King Jr. identified what we need in his sermon *On Being a Good Neighbor*, a population of citizens taking upon themselves unenforceable obligations spurred on by altruism. Government will continue to fail for the reason Rev. Dr. King stated, but also because it is not entrepreneurial.

Entrepreneurs are the ones who create new wealth that, in turn, results in new jobs. It will take altruistic entrepreneurs, motivated by unenforceable obligations, and unfettered by political strings, to propagate an economic surge for our less privileged brothers and sisters. The true solution to our impoverished communities, regardless of skin color, will only be found in the same fundamental principle that led to our nation's overall success, free-market enterprise.

To enable impoverished citizens with the ability to create and successfully operate their own businesses, I envision a revival. I see a movement originated and led by Christians in the private sector, motivated and guided by a radical altruism rooted in a Christian attitude of self-sacrifice. This is a vision of a free-market revival in the impoverished neighborhoods of our communities.

CHAPTER 21

FREE-MARKET REVIVAL

"Turn, O Lord! How long? Have compassion on your servants!
Satisfy us in the morning with your steadfast love, so that we may
rejoice and be glad all our days. Make us glad as many days as you
have afflicted us, and as many years as we have seen evil. Let your
work be manifest to your servants, and your glorious power to their
children. Let the favor of the Lord our God be upon us, and prosper
for us the work of our hands—O prosper the work of our hands!"

Psalm 90:13–17, NRSV, from a prayer of Moses, the man of God who
led the people of Israel out of slavery to the promised land of freedom.

God has given me what He has in trust to make of it a contribution
to the world far greater than money can for myself."

George Washington Carver, March 24, 1925

A TIME FOR DOING

Most adults in low-income segregated communities are employed.[110]
Most of them work hard for a living. Although they feel the sting of
discrimination, they do not participate in riots or looting. The schools
they attended, and their children attend, may be substandard, but

they have the same capacity to learn and work, and the same desire for a better life for themselves and their children, as those living in other more well-to-do neighborhoods. They hope for what they do not have, the wherewithal to raise themselves and their families out of their lower estate to participate in the freedom and prosperity they perceive other Americans enjoy. Their weekly struggle to make ends meet while having to worry about the safety and security of their family, home, and possessions, makes it difficult to envision a way out of their circumstances.

Not all people have the initiative and desire to start and manage a business, but in any given community, there is a fair percentage of individuals that will welcome the opportunity if you offer them the knowledge, resources, and mentoring. Not all individuals may succeed in the attempt, but most can thrive given the proper support. Those that thrive will need employees, and within their community, they will find many who want to join with them to help make their new local business succeed.

Events of 2020 have helped bring to light the loss of productive abilities in the United States due largely to US corporations moving their manufacturing facilities offshore, particularly to China. Within our disadvantaged communities exists a vast latent capacity for productive enterprise. A well of potential commerce and prosperity languishes, waiting for the right combination of inspiration, innovation, and investment. Meanwhile, governments and private entities expend tens of billions of dollars merely maintaining the status quo.

I believe the time has come to stop expecting a new result to spring forth from the collective halls and assemblies of government after over fifty years of failed programs and promises. I also believe we have had enough complaints and demands for change, generalities about what and how to change without concrete plans and meaningful action. I sense a desire among many Americans to stop thinking and talking of the need to do something, but instead get about doing.

STARTING WITH THE HEART

The changes that need to take place are not simple or easy. Before physical change can happen, attitudes, hearts, and minds must change. These changes need to occur throughout society, outside, as well as within marginalized communities. Those on the outside require an attitude of altruism. More than just knowing there is a problem, hearts need to feel compelled and possess a desire to serve and sacrifice for the sake of others.

Inside, individuals must recognize change will only come from within. Negative and defeatist attitudes need to be replaced by positive can-do enthusiasm. We must reject the concepts of victim status and Uncle Tom. The victim attitude believes someone else needs to fix my problem. Even if your problem can be traced to blaming someone else, only you can raise yourself up.

The Uncle Tom concept mistakes the principles that one embraces that leads to prosperity as a white sellout. The economic principles and benefits of a free economy belong to all people of all races. By embracing those principles, one makes the statement that he or she is just as worthy to enjoy the privileges they yield as anyone else.

The inability of past programs to succeed result from a failure to recognize the need for the crucial change in attitudes. Government cannot accomplish this. The ability to imbue individuals with an altruistic resolve resides in the same source of courage and strength that sustained Rev. Dr. Martin Luther King, a deep and abiding faith in Jesus Christ. Just as great creative and productive power resides dormant in distressed communities, a great well of power to change hearts and minds lies fallow in the Christian church. A renewal of society requires a new awakening in the church to this great cause.

A first step should establish interconnectedness within the church. Rather than gather in protest and conflict, congregations need to come together from all sectors of the city and join in prayer. As we gather, we should consider what Paul tells the Colossians:

"But now you must get rid of all such things—anger, wrath, malice, slander, and abusive language from your mouth. Do not lie to one another, seeing that you have stripped off the old self with its practices and have clothed yourselves with the new self, which is being renewed in knowledge according to the image of its creator. In that renewal, there is no longer Greek and Jew, circumcised and uncircumcised, barbarian, Scythian, slave and free; but Christ is all and in all! As God's chosen ones, holy and beloved, clothe yourselves with compassion, kindness, humility, meekness, and patience. Bear with one another and, if anyone has a complaint against another, forgive each other; just as the Lord has forgiven you, so you also must forgive. Above all, clothe yourselves with love, which binds everything together in perfect harmony." (Colossians 3:8–14, NRSV)

Cultivating that binding love is the key that refines hearts to let down the walls within us that cause the hesitation and wariness that hinders us from answering the Samaritan call.

Gathering should build unity and harmony. We do not come together to discuss who to vote for or what party to support. We do not need to garner support of any national politician or political party that will only create division. Although my appeal here goes out to the Christian church, any gathering should be welcoming to all who come with a sincere desire to aid in the cause, without creating division or disharmony. We become united in the bond of love and fellowship for a common purpose.

That purpose is to invigorate those neighborhoods that have suffered from the consequences of segregation based upon not just skin color, but upon income status. That invigoration would come in the form of start-up funding, expertise, and personal involvement of entrepreneurs to guide and counsel residents of disadvantaged neighborhoods who have the desire to start their own business enterprises. The specifics of how that would be organized will come to light as the larger Church community comes together in prayer seeking Providential guidance.

We must recognize the fundamental problems that bring about the distressing symptoms of poverty and engage in the difficult task of confessing our complicity with those problems. We need to acknowledge the breakdown of families, the decline of morality, and lost value placed on the sanctity of marriage and parenting.

When we gather and pray and confess and forgive one another, we all do so in complete humility. No one can claim greater righteousness than others. From our humble perspective, we are all the same in God's eyes. I can promise with all certainty, that if done in honest sincerity, plumbing the depths of each of our failings, the power and Spirit of God will be overwhelming in the hearts of those participating.

As we bare our souls, we recognize that we join in a great cause. We pray for help in this great cause. We pray for the workers to come into the fields. We pray for needed resources and support. If we offer our prayers in humble confidence and faith in the grace and power of almighty God, in the name of the only self-sacrificing savior Jesus Christ, then God will supply all things required to fulfill His purposes.

CHAPTER 22

POSSIBILITIES

"God who gave us life gave us liberty. Can the liberties of a nation be secure when we have removed a conviction that these liberties are the gift of God? Indeed I tremble for my country when I reflect that God is just, that his justice cannot sleep forever."

Thomas Jefferson, 1774 & 1785[111]

"This is the beginning of a new day. God has given me this day to use as I will. I can waste it or use it for good. What I do today is important, because I am exchanging a day of my life for it. When tomorrow comes, this day will be gone forever, leaving in its place something that I have traded for it. I want it to be gain, not loss; good, not evil; success not failure, in order that I shall not regret the price I paid for it."

Dr. Heartsill Wilson, *A Salesman's Prayer*, 1954

".... for God all things are possible."

Mark 10:27, NRSV

THE UNTIMELY DEATH OF MY BROTHER is heartbreaking. Each death caused by COVID-19 is tragic. In the same way each death of our youth and young men and women who die by violence in our streets, neighborhoods, and homes represents a tragedy. I also reflect often on the ultimate sacrifices made by many from our nation in the defense of freedoms for our nation, as well as others around the world. Each premature death represents a tragedy.

I owe it to my brother, and we all owe it to each person who has suffered and died, regardless of their circumstances, that their premature passing from this life is not in vain. Out of tragedy comes the possibility for positive outcomes. There are many lessons we can learn that will provide better guidance in the future. There are many things we can do to right past wrongs and make us as a society and nation stronger and more productive. This book merely scratches the surface of possibilities.

I first conceived of how I would end this book before there was a Coronavirus pandemic. Before then, we were clearly a nation deeply divided politically. In a perverse way, the virus provided an opportunity for our nation. I heard other people sensing the same possibility of ultimate positive outcomes as we came out of the tragic situation of COVID-19. The nation coming together politically and spiritually in a positive light infused an optimism in me as I first drafted my conclusion to this book.

Then just over a month after my brother's passing, racial protest, and violence broke out in response to the death of George Floyd. The divide in our nation not only returned to the forefront, it also seemed to widen. Every tragedy that could be a motivation for change and unity now appears to become a political weapon used to deepen and widen the gaping wound of division.

This book discusses the history and causes of the divide between black and white America. Factual books and written testimonies of freed slaves in the 18th and 19th centuries helped fuel the abolitionist movement that ultimately led to the passage of the 14th Amendment in the year 1868. That amendment granted the right of citizenship for all men and women regardless of skin pigmentation who were born or naturalized in the United States. Two years later, the 15th Amendment granted black men the right to vote.

It has been over 150 years since black men were given the right to vote, and well over fifty years since official assurance of that right became effective. How long should we wait to act on the lingering inequities we still see? As a nation, I do not believe we can bear to wait any longer. As Paul told the Corinthians, "now is the acceptable time; see, now is the day of salvation!" We need not wait for a certain person or party to be elected. The power to do good has always been in the possession of the American public, within the hands of the Christian church.

I talk about the poverty of party politics. Also, about the loss of an objective unbiased news media. Many voters get their news from common media sources. The news sources get their "facts" from politicians who are influenced by party loyalties. One hundred and sixty years ago, this same type of disconnected bias helped lead the United States into the Civil War that cost more American lives than any other war we have fought.

I discussed the impetus that started the Civil War as the election of Abraham Lincoln to the Presidency. Lincoln was not a radical, but Democrats of his day portrayed him as such. Near the end of that terrible Civil War, Lincoln admonished that there should be no vengeance. There were to be no punishments meted out by the northern victors upon the vanquished South. Healing would require forgiveness. Before he could carry out his plan for reconciliation, he was assassinated by intractable souls who could not forgive.

Forgiveness is a hallmark of the United States. After World War II, the United States helped rebuild Japan and Europe including Germany. Japan and Germany have been significant trading partners for years.

Vietnam now also trades with the US, and we are their second-largest trading partner. We as a nation and society have the ability to forgive. This reflects our Christian tradition. There are many societies in this world who are unable to forgive.

Jesus calls everyone who would follow him to begin with two things. The first is repentance. Sincerely reflecting on what we think, do, say, and believe, and remove or change those things that are contrary to an honest and faithful life in Christ. The second is forgiveness. Forgiveness requires we bare our soul to God and those we wronged and sincerely ask for forgiveness. It also requires that we forgive those who have wronged us.

I speak a lot in this book about the types of fiscal decisions that are beneficial when facing a crisis, and those that are not. Before that can happen, I am convinced that politicians and citizens on all sides in our nation need to stop and take time to consider what Jesus taught us as necessary. To best address our crises and adversaries we need to be united in our desire to act in the best interest of all in our nation. The best result for our children and grandchildren will come about if we first join together in a prayerful spirit of repentance, confession, and forgiveness to heal the divisions and find unified Providential guidance.

The positive potential in our nation is greater than any other nation in history. We have a choice to make. On one hand, we may simply choose to continue on our present path; a divided nation spiraling downward in a sea of debt, moral bankruptcy, and inattention to those who seek our downfall.

On the other hand, we have an opportunity to create a united nation resolved to overcome our disparities and strive to release the full potential of American ingenuity against present and future crises. An opportunity to look beyond the dismal present to see the great opportunities that our narrow perspectives hide from view. To envision a society that nurtures a positive environment for all citizens to receive the knowledge and skills, motivation, and confidence to pursue and benefit from their dreams, innovations, and constructive efforts.

To unlock the power of the United States of America to address any crisis, we need to avoid top-down dictates formulated by a very few individuals in positions of high authority in the federal government guided by narrow perspectives. We unleash this power by enabling millions of thinking and innovative Americans to invent and devise solutions in thousands of different ways, guided by sound principles of free markets, productivity increase, Christian morals, and the beneficent hand of Providence. Do this, and the positive possibilities for our nation are limitless.

The time has come to expose the false narrative of the Rhetoric and return to the promise of the ideals the founders of this nation expressed well over 200 years ago. When we recognize and return to promote and protect the most fundamental ideal of individual freedom for all citizens guided in the righteousness of a loving Creator, then we shall see the possibilities of a new age of enlightenment, awakening, and prosperity.

Amen.

ABOUT THE AUTHOR

JOHN WHITE began exploring for metal deposits in the western United States after receiving a master's degree from the University of Arizona focused on economic geology. The economic downturn of 1982 led him to relocate to New Mexico where he worked for many years in underground and surface silver, copper, and gold mines. The ups and downs of the mining industry led John to transition to construction in the late 1990's.

John has held executive positions in three corporations. Simultaneously, he has served as a City Commissioner, governor's business advisor, university adjunct professor, as well as other voluntary roles in government, civic, professional, and church organizations. Mr. White's wide-ranging background provides a unique perspective that colors the topics of his writing.

Mr. White presently manages projects including controlled blasting operations for a construction company. He also co-owns and manages a separate restoration business. John and his wife Mabel live in Albuquerque, New Mexico, with three of their six children and five of their seven grandchildren living nearby.

ENDNOTES

1   All Bible quotations are from *The Holy Bible: New Revised Standard Version*. Nashville: Thomas Nelson Publishers, 1989.

2   It is inaccurate to state this in the converse, "Your rights end where my rights begin." This is contrary to the self-sacrificial principle Jesus taught commonly referred to as the Golden Rule, "Do unto others as you would have them do unto you." Those who push their own boundaries of freedom at the expense of others often cause the state to step in and restrict freedoms in one direction or the other. This results in incremental losses of freedom for all citizens.

3   Bowden, Mark. 2013. "'Idiot', 'Yahoo', 'Original Gorilla': How Lincoln Was Dissed in His Day." *The Atlantic*, June 2013 issue.

4   American Battlefield Trust, Evidence for The Unpopular Mr. Lincoln, battlefields.org/learn/articles/evidence-unpopular-mr-lincoln.

5   Fehrenbacher, Don E., *The Anti-Lincoln Tradition, Journal of the Abraham Lincoln Association*, Volume 4, Issue 1, 1982, pp6-28.

6   For example: Lay, Benjamin, All Slave Keepers that Keep the Innocent in Bondage (Philadelphia: Printed for the Author, 1737)

7   Another example: The Liberator, an abolitionist journal, the first issue published in January 1831, by William Lloyd Garrison, funded by prominent New York City evangelical businessmen.

8   A third example: Bourne, George, A Condensed Anti-slavery Bible Argument; By a Citizen of Virginia, (New York: S.W. Benedict, 1845)

9   Solzhenitsyn, Aleksandr, May, 10, 1983, quoted from his acceptance speech given in London when he was awarded the Templeton Prize for Progress in Religion.

10 Zingales, Luigi, 2012, *A Capitalism for the People*. New York: Basic Books, 2012. See Mr. Zingales' chapter on The Need for a Market-Based Ethics.

11 "The Legislation Placing "In God We Trust" on National Currency, US House of Representatives: History, Art & Archives"; history.house.gov 1955-07-11. Retrieved 2017-05-13. (Wikipedia, 2019-06-25).

12 Wikipedia (2019), Importance of Religion by Country, information provided in the article based on a 2009 worldwide Gallup poll.

13 Eldred, Ken, *The Integrated Life*. Montrose, CO: Manna Ventures, LLC 2010, p. 52-78.

14 Panic of 1837, Wikipedia, last edit date June 14, 2020.

15 Friedman, Milton and Anna Jacobson Schwartz. *A Monetary History of the United States*, 1867-1960. Princeton: Princeton University Press, 9th paperback edition, 1993, p. 419.

16 Douglas A. Irwin. 2012. "Gold Sterilization and the Recession of 1937-1938." *Financial History Review 19*, p. 249-267 doi: 10.1017/S0968565012000236

17 Recession of 1981-82, written as of November 22, 2013, Federal Reserve History. https://www.federalreservehistory. org/essays/recession_of_1981_82#:~:text=By%20October%20 1982%2C%20inflation%20had,Federal%20Reserve%20 Bank%20of%20St.

18 Ruffing, Kathy. November 15, 2011. "The Composition of Past Deficit Reduction Packages – and Lessons for the Next One, Center on Budget and Policy Priorities." https://www.cbpp.org/research/the-composition-of-past-deficit-reduction-packages-and-lessons-for-the-next-one

19 Mitchell, B., *International Historical Statistics: Americas, 1750-2000*. Basingstoke: Palgrave Macmillan, 2003.

20 Maddison, Angus. 2001. "The World Economy: A Millennial Perspective." The Development Centre of the Organization for Economic Co-Operation and Development.

21 Based on IMF data thru 2019.

22 See: "Total population, both sexes combined (thousands)." UNdata. United Nations Statistics Division. 17 June 2019. Retrieved 30 July 2019.

23 See: https://data.worldbank.org/indicator/NY.GDP.PCAP.PP.CD Most recent year 2019.

24 The entities and their per capita GDP PPPs from World Bank data for 2019: Macau, 129,103; Luxembourg, 121,293; Singapore, 101,376; Qatar, 96,491; Ireland, 88,241; Cayman Islands, 72,481; Switzerland, 70,989; United Arab Emirates, 69,904; Norway, 66,832.

25 See: forbes.com/billionaires/ as of September 28, 2020

26 Worstall, Tom. June 1, 2013. "Astonishing Numbers: America's Poor Still Live Better Than Most of the Rest of Humanity. *Forbes Magazine*. https://www.forbes.com/sites/timworstall/2013/06/01/astonishing-numbers-americas-poor-still-live-better-than-most-of-the-rest-of-humanity/#5d29f62e54ef

27 Gross Domestic Philanthropy: An international analysis of GDP, tax and giving, January 2016, a Charities Aid Foundation publication.

28 This is based on a quick calculation made using 1.35%, the difference in giving between the United States and Switzerland expressed as a percent of GDP, times the per capita GDP PPP

value for the United States starting in 1980, and amortized over 40 years to 2019 using a rate of 3.73%. The 3.73% is the average historical growth rate of the U.S. GDP PPP over the last 40 years. Baseline data per World Bank estimates per note 21, and Charities Aid Foundation per note 25.

29   US Census data. https://www2.census.gov/library/ publications/1949/compendia/hist_stats_1789-1945/hist_ stats_1789-1945-chP.pdf

30   Amadeo, Kimberly. December 31, 2019. "US Federal Budget Breakdown." thebalance.com. Percentages calculated using figures cited in the article.

31   Marx, Karl, and Frederick Engels, *Manifesto of the Communist Party*, English Edition, 1888.

32   Reed, Lawrence W. November 18, 2012. "Great Myths of the Great Depression." Foundation for Economic Education.

33   FDR's Disputed Legacy, *Time*, February 1, 1982, p. 23.

34   Johnson, Paul, *A History of the American People* (New York: HarperCollins Publishers, 1997), p. 741.

35   Hu, Zuliu, Mohsin S. Khan. 1997. "Why is China Growing So Fast?." International Monetary Fund Working Paper 96/75, edited and refined by Rozlyn Coleman for version presented as Economic Issues Series No. 8. The edited version was used as the source for this book.

36   Sources of Data for Charts in Figures 1 and 2: www.thebalance. com; www.fred.stlouisfed.org/series.ASPUS; www.multpl. com>us-median-income>table>by-year

37   See tradingeconomics.com/country-list/government-debt-to-gdp; or worldpopulationreview.com/countries/countries-by-national-debt;

38   Quote from speech given on the floor of the House of Representatives by David Crockett. The speech is recorded in the book by Edward S. Ellis, 1884, *The Life of Colonel David Crockett,* (Philadelphia: Porter & Coates), page 138.

39   Ray, Brian D. Research Facts on Homeschooling. March 23,

2020. nheri.org/research-facts-on-homeschooling/

40   *Washington Post* Editorial Board. April 23, 2020. "The lessons from Trump's Reckless Recommendation of Hydroxychloroquine." *Washington Post.* https://www. washingtonpost.com/opinions/global-opinions/the-lessons- from-trumps-reckless-recommendation-of-hydroxychloroquine /2020/04/23/4626c4ce-84bc-11ea-ae26-989cfce1c7c7_story.html

41   Bendavid, Eran, Bianca Mulaney, Neeraj Sood, Soleil Shah, Emilia Ling, Rebecca Bromley-Dulfano, Cara Lai, Zoe Weissberg, Rodrigo Saavedra-Walker, Jim Tedrow, Dona Tversky, Andrew Bogan, Thomas Kupiec, Daniel Eichner, Ribhav Gupta, John P.A. Ioannidis, Jay Bhattacharya. April 11, 2020. Covid-19 Antibody Seroprevalence in Santa Clara County, California. https://www.courthousenews.com/wp- content/uploads/2020/04/Stanford.pdf

42   Ealy, Henry, Michael McEnvoy, Daniel Chong, John Nowicki, Monica Sava, Sandeep Gupta, David White, James Jordan, Daniel Simon, Paul Anderson. October 12, 2020. COVID-19 Data Collection, Comorbidity & Federal Law: A Historical Perspective, in Science, Public Health Policy, and The Law, Volume 2:4-22.

43   Reynolds, Sharon. January 26, 2021. "Lasting Immunity Found After Recovery from COVID-19. National Institutes of Health, NIH Research Matters. https://www.nih.gov/news-events/ nih-research-matters/lasting-immunity-found-after-recovery- covid-19

44   CDC Morbidity and Mortality Weekly Report (MMWR) March 5, 2021, Hobbs CV, Drobeniuc J, Kittle T, et al. Estimated SARS-CoV-2 Seroprevalence Among Persons Aged <18 Years — Mississippi, May–September 2020. MMWR Morb Mortal Wkly Rep 2021;70:312–315. DOI: http://dx.doi. org/10.15585/mmwr.mm7009a4external icon.

45   CDC Tables KCWK1_HR_2017. Deaths, percent of total deaths, and death rates for the 15 leading causes of death in 5-year age groups, by race and Hispanic origin, and sex: United States, 2017. www.cdc.gov/ncha/nvss/mortality/1cwk1_

hr.htm

46   Samuelsohn, Darren. April 17, 2016. Could Trump Be Impeached Shortly After He Takes Office? *Politico*. https://www.politico.eu/article/could-donald-trump-be-impeached-shortly-after-he-takes-office-us-presidential-election-2016-american-president-impeachment/

47   Gold, Matea. January 20, 2017. "The Campaign To Impeach President Trump Has Begun." *The Washington Post*. https://www.washingtonpost.com/news/post-politics/wp/2017/01/20/the-campaign-to-impeach-president-trump-has-begun/

48   Judicial Watch Press Release, May 20, 2020. Judicial Watch Lawsuit Forces Declassification and Release of 'Electronic Communication' Used to Launch Obama Administration's Spy Operation on President Trump's 2016 Campaign.

49   Felten, Eric. November 17, 2020. "The FBI Spying Denial That Never Grows Cold, Real Clear Investigations." https://www.realclearinvestigations.com/articles/2020/11/17/the_denial_of_fbi_spying_that_never_got_old_126035.html

50   Solomon, John. April 1, 2019 updated February 19, 2020. "Joe Biden's Ukrainian Nightmare: A Closed Probe Is Revived. *The Hill*. https://thehill.com/opinion/white-house/436816-joe-bidens-2020-ukrainian-nightmare-a-closed-probe-is-revived

51   Meyer, Katie. August 6, 2020. The partisan conflict behind a quest to purge up to 800,000 voters from Pa's rolls, PBS website, https://whyy.org/articles/the-partisan-conflict-behind-a-quest-to-purge-up-to-800000-voters-from-pa-s-rolls/

52   Lott, John R., Jr. August 3, 2020. Why do most countries ban mail-in ballots?: They have seen massive vote fraud problems, Crime Prevention Research Center report, see the appendix: voting rules by country.

53   Kengor, Paul, November 28, 2020, Pennsylvania Bombshell: Biden 99.4% v. Trump 0.6%, Special Report in The American Spectator

54   November 6, 2020, Preliminary Statement of the OAS Electoral Observation Mission for the November 3, 2020 General

Elections in the United States of America

55 Ball, Molly. February 15, 2021. "The Secret History of the Shadow Campaign That Saved the 2020 Election." *Time Magazine*

56 Biden Voter Messaging Survey Analysis, by Media Research Center. https://cdn.mrc.org/TPC-MRC+Biden+Voter+Messaging+Survey+Analysis+Nov+2020_final.pdf

57 https://Hereistheevidence.com

58 Byrne, Patrick. 2021. "The Deep Rig: How Election Fraud Cost Donald J. Trump the White House, By a Man Who did not Vote for Him." (Deep Capture, LLC)

59 https://2020evidence.org

60 https://navarroreport.com

61 Jesus speaking to the scribes from Jerusalem, from Mark 12:24, NRSV.

62 Reuters. April 2, 2021. "Illegal US Border Crossings Surge to Highest Level in Two DECADES. See https://www.rt.com/usa/520013-border-crossers-record-mexico-biden/

63 Niyazov, Sukhayl. January 23, 2021. "Cancelling the Keystone Pipeline Is a Mistake, Human Events." https://humanevents.com/2021/01/23/canceling-the-keystone-pipeline-is-a-mistake/

64 Brown, Jerrod. August 4, 2007. "Father-Absent Homes: Implications for Criminal Justice and Mental Health Professionals" Minnesota Psychological Association mnpsych.org

65 Unitedfamilies.org/child-development/fatherlessness-poverty-and-crime/

66 Janique Kroese, Wim Bernasco, Aart C. Liefbroer & JanRouwendal. 2020. "Growing Up in Single-Parent Families and the Criminal Involvement of Adolescents: A Systematic Review." *Psychology, Crime & Law*. DOI: 10.1080/1068316X.2020.1774589. June, 11, 2020. https://doi.org/10.1080/1068316X.2020.1774589

67 Fagan, Patrick. March 17,1995. "The Real Root Causes of

Violent Crime: The Breakdown of Marriage, Family, and Community." heritage.org/crime-and-justice/report

68   Hymowitz, Kay. December 3, 2012. "The Real, Complex Connection Between Single-Parent Families and Crime." Theatlantic.com/sexes/archive/2012

69   Raley, Kelly R., Megan M. Sweeney, and Danielle Wondra. 2015. "The Growing Racial and Ethnic Divide in U.S. Marriage Patterns." *Future Child*. 2015 Fall; 25(2): 89-109. ncbi.nlm.nih. gov/pmc/articles/PMC4850739/

70   Pew Research Center, Social & Demographic Trends, June 27, 2016. "On Views of Race and Inequality, Blacks and Whites Are Worlds Apart." Pewsocialtrends.org/2016/06/27/

71   Zeng, Jennifer, and Hannah Cai. June 5, 2021, "NewsBreak App Founded, Controlled, and Backed by Chinese Entities." *Epoch Times*.

72   Marx, Karl, 1845, Theses on Feuerbach, item XI.

73   "Why Are the Twin Cities So Segregated?" February, 2015. Institute on Metropolitan Opportunity, University of Minnesota Law School, Minneapolis.

74   US Census estimates for the state of Minnesota in 2019.

75   CDC Tables KCWK1_HR_2017. Deaths, percent of total deaths, and death rates for the 15 leading causes of death in 5-year age groups, by race and Hispanic origin, and sex: United States, 2017. www.cdc.gov/ncha/nvss/mortality/1cwk1_hr.htm

76   CDC Tables KCWK1_HR_2017. Deaths, percent of total deaths, and death rates for the 15 leading causes of death in 5-year age groups, by race and Hispanic origin, and sex: United States, 2017. www.cdc.gov/ncha/nvss/mortality/1cwk1_hr.htm

77   FBI: Expanded Homicide Data Tables. Ucr.fbi.gov/crime-in-the-us/2018

78   Brown, Jerrod. August 4, 2007. "Father-Absent Homes: Implications for Criminal Justice and Mental Health Professionals." Minnesota Psychological Association. mnpsych.org

79   Unitedfamilies.org/child-development/fatherlessness-poverty-and-crime/

80   Janique Kroese, Wim Bernasco, Aart C. Liefbroer & JanRouwendal. 2020. "Growing Up in Single-Parent Families and the Criminal Involvement of Adolescents: A Systematic Review." *Psychology, Crime & Law*, DOI: 10.1080/1068316X.2020.1774589. Published online June, 11 2020. https://doi.org/10.1080/1068316X.2020.1774589

81   Fagan, Patrick. March 17, 1995. The Real Root Causes of Violent Crime: The Breakdown of Marriage, Family, and Community, heritage.org/crime-and-justice/report

82   Hymowitz, Kay. December 3, 2012. "The Real, Complex Connection Between Single-Parent Families and Crime." Theatlantic.com/sexes/archive/2012

83   Raley, Kelly R., Megan M. Sweeney, and Danielle Wondra. 2015. "The Growing Racial and Ethnic Divide in U.S. Marriage Patterns." *Future Child.* 2015 Fall; 25(2): 89–109. ncbi.nlm.nih.gov/pmc/articles/PMC4850739/

84   Pew Research Center, Social & Demographic Trends. June 27, 2016. "On Views of Race and Inequality, Blacks and Whites Are Worlds Apart." Pewsocialtrends.org/2016/06/27/

85   Raley, Kelly R., et al.

86   Madisa, 2017, *Bleed the Same.* Popular Christian singer Mandisa recorded on Capitol Records this song built on the saying "we all bleed the same." I recommend this song to citizens concerned about racial divisions.

87   Wilcox, W. Bradford. 2009. "The Evolution of Divorce." nationalaffairs.com/publications/detail/the-evolution-of-divorce.

88   History.com Editors. "Jim Crow Laws." History. https://www.history.com/topics/early-20th-century-us/jim-crow-laws

89   Hankin-Redmon, Eric. "Near North African American Community, Minneapolis." MNopedia, Minnesota Historical Society. http://www.mnopedia.org/place/near-north-african-

american-community-minneapolis (Accessed July 28, 2020).

90   Gal, Shayanne, Andy Kiersz, Michelle Mark, Ruobing Su, and Marguerite Ward. July 8, 2020. "26 Simple Charts to Show Friends and Family Who Aren't Convinced Racism Is Still a Problem in America." *Business Insider*. businessinsider.com/us-systemic-racism-in-charts-graphs-data-202006

91   Maloney, Thomas N. 2001. "African Americans in the Twentieth Century, Economic History Association." https://eh.net/encyclopedia/african-americans-in-the-twentieth-century/

92   Desilver, Drew. August 23, 2013. Black Unemployment Rate Is Consistently Twice That of Whites, Pew Research Center, https://www.pewresearch.org/fact-tank/2013/08/21/through-good-times-and-bad-black-unemployment-is-consistently-double-that-of-whites/

93   Maloney, Thomas N. 2001. "African Americans in the Twentieth Century, Economic History Association." https://eh.net/encyclopedia/african-americans-in-the-twentieth-century/

94   Langan, Patrick A. May 1991. "Race of Prisoners Admitted to State and Federal Institutions, 1926-86." NCJ-125618, US Department of Justice, Bureau of Justice Statistics

95   Buchholtz, Katharina. June 14, 2019. "Black Incarceration Rates Are Dropping in the U.S." https://www.statista.com/chart/18376/us-incarceration-rates-by-sex-and-race-ethnic-origin/

96   Raley, Kelly R, et al., 2015

97   Raley, Kelly R., et al., ibid.

98   See: blacklivesmatter.com

99   From website: blacklivesmatter.com, *What We Believe*, August 5, 2020.

100 Polumbo, Brad. July 7, 2020. "Is Black Lives Matter Marxist? No and Yes, Foundation for Economic Education." website: https://fee.org/articles/is-black-lives-matter-marxist-no-and-yes/

101 See: M4bl.org/

102 See: whitesforracialequity.org/

103 See: https://www.influencewatch.org/movement/black-lives-matter/

104 See: secure.actblue.com

105 See: Ballotpedia.org/Presidential_voting_trends_in_Minnesota

106 See: en.wikipedia.org/wiki/List_of_mayors_of_Minneapolis

107 See: https://blackdemographics.com/culture/black-politics/

108 King, Martin Luther Jr. 1963. *Strength to Love*. Minneapolis: Fortress Press. I highly recommend this book to every concerned American regardless of your politics, race, religion etc.

109 King, 1963, Chapter 3, On Being a Good Neighbor. See also The Holy Bible, Luke 10:25–36

110 I assume based upon unemployment statistics for low-income black communities discussed in this cited article, given unemployment rates for these black communities between 11% and 20%, that the employment rate may be somewhere around 75% to 85%. See: Perry, Andre M. June 26, 2019, Black workers are being left behind by full employment, posted in The Brookings Institute blog, The Avenue at https://www.brookings.edu/blog/the-avenue/2019/06/26/black-workers-are-being-left-behind-by-full-employment/

111 Jefferson, Thomas, Quotation included on Panel Three in the Jefferson Memorial in Washington, DC. The quote is an aggregate of select quotes from two of Jefferson's writings: 1) A Summary View of the Rights of British America, 1774; and 2) Notes on the State of Virginia, Query XVIII, published in France 1785.

www.ingramcontent.com/pod-product-compliance
Lightning Source LLC
Chambersburg PA
CBHW031504270326
41930CB00006B/247